Mastery of Your Anxiety and

MW01011928

EDITOR-IN-CHIEF

David H. Barlow, Ph.D.

SCIENTIFIC
ADIVISORY BOARD

Anne Marie Albano, Ph.D.

Jack M. Gorman, M.D.

Peter Nathan, Ph.D.

Bonnie Spring, Ph.D.

Paul Salkovskis, Ph.D.

G. Terence Wilson, Ph.D.

John R. Weisz, Ph.D.

Mastery of Your Anxiety and Worry

SECOND EDITION

Workbook

Michelle G. Craske • David H. Barlow

OXFORD

UNIVERSITY PRESS

2006

OXFORD

UNIVERSITY PRESS

Oxford University Press, Inc., publishes works that further
Oxford University's objective of excellence
in research, scholarship, and education.

Oxford   New York
Auckland   Cape Town   Dar es Salaam   Hong Kong   Karachi
Kuala Lumpur   Madrid   Melbourne   Mexico City   Nairobi
New Delhi   Shanghai   Taipei   Toronto

With offices in
Argentina   Austria   Brazil   Chile   Czech Republic   France   Greece
Guatemala   Hungary   Italy   Japan   Poland   Portugal   Singapore
South Korea   Switzerland   Thailand   Turkey   Ukraine   Vietnam

Copyright © 2006 by Oxford University Press, Inc.

Published by Oxford University Press, Inc.
198 Madison Avenue, New York, New York 10016
www.oup.com

Oxford is a registered trademark of Oxford University Press

All rights reserved. No part of this publication may be reproduced,
stored in a retrieval system, or transmitted, in any form or by any means,
electronic, mechanical, photocopying, recording, or otherwise,
without the prior permission of Oxford University Press.

ISBN-13: 978-0-19-530001-7 (pbk.)

21

Printed in the United States of America
on acid-free paper

About Treatments That Work™

One of the most difficult problems confronting patients with various disorders and diseases is finding the best help available. Everyone is aware of friends or family who have sought treatment from a seemingly reputable practitioner, only to find out later from another doctor that the original diagnosis was wrong or that the treatments recommended were inappropriate, or perhaps even harmful. Most patients, or family members, address this problem by reading everything they can about their symptoms, seeking out information on the Internet, or aggressively "asking around" to tap knowledge from friends and acquaintances. Governments and health care policymakers are also aware that people in need don't always get the best treatments—something they refer to as "variability in health care practices."

Now health care systems around the world are attempting to correct this variability by introducing "evidence-based practice." This simply means that it is in everyone's interest that patients get the most up-to-date and effective care for a particular problem. Health care policymakers have also recognized that it is very useful to give consumers of health care as much information as possible, so that they can make intelligent decisions in a collaborative effort to improve health and mental health. This series, "*Treatments That Work™*," is designed to accomplish just that. Only the latest and most effective interventions for particular problems are described in user-friendly language. To be included in this series, each treatment program must pass the highest standards of evidence available, as determined by a scientific advisory board. Thus, when individuals suffering from these problems, or their family members, seek out an expert clinician who is familiar with these interventions and decides that they are appropriate, they will have confidence that they are receiving the best care available. Of course, only your health care professional can decide on the right mix of treatments for you.

This particular program presents the latest version of a cognitive-behavioral treatment for generalized anxiety disorder that has proven effectiveness and was developed in our own Center for Anxiety and Related Disorders at Boston University. In this program, you will learn skills to cope effectively with the chronic tension, irritability, difficulty sleeping, and constant, uncontrollable worry that make life so miserable for people with this disorder. This program is most effectively applied by working in collaboration with your clinician.

David H. Barlow, Editor-in-Chief,
Treatments That Work™
Boston, Massachusetts

Contents

Chapter 1

Is This Program Right for You? The Nature of Generalized Anxiety

Goals

- To understand the characteristics of generalized anxiety disorder

- To learn the difference between normal worry and abnormal worry

- To understand what this program is and what it will involve

- To determine whether or not this program is right for you

What is generalized anxiety disorder (GAD)? There are two core features of generalized anxiety. The first is excessive worry about things that are unlikely to happen, or, if they were to happen, would be much more manageable than worriers think. Examples include worrying about the health of one's family, worrying about not getting everything done on time at work or at home, and worrying about not being good enough as a parent or as a husband or wife. Worry is almost always about events that could happen in the future, and therefore, it is characterized by "What if" types of statements.

Excessive worry is typically difficult to stop, or is experienced as if it is out of control. At times, you might try to resist worrying because it seems that it is excessive, abnormal, or at least not much fun. At other times, you might feel that if you do not worry, something terrible might really happen, as if the worrying serves some kind of protective, or even superstitious, function. Sometimes people who are chronic worriers report that they become nervous if things seem to be going well in their lives, as if they are experiencing the "calm before the storm." In other words, there might be a tendency to worry, even if there is nothing to worry about, because you are so used to worrying. We will talk about the quality of this type of worry later in this chapter and other chapters.

The second core feature of generalized anxiety is a generally high level of physical tension, nervousness, or a feeling of being "uptight" or "high-strung." The physical tension is likely to result from excessive and chronic worrying. In addition, high levels of tension add to excessive worrying, since it is hard to be worried when feeling physically relaxed. Obviously, the high level of physical tension and the excessive worrying feed off of each other, creating a vicious cycle. It is this cycle that the program described in this workbook is designed to break. The physical tension produces a variety of symptoms, such as muscular tension and soreness, headaches, difficulty sleeping, poor concentration, diarrhea and frequent urination, and restlessness and general difficulty relaxing.

With the combination of excessive worry and high levels of physical tension, it's not hard to understand why you might feel anxious, irritable, tired, and generally distressed. If you are a chronic worrier and are overly concerned about everything that could go wrong, if you find yourself exhausted at the end of the day from driving yourself too hard, and yet wonder what you have accomplished and how you are going to get tomorrow's work done, this program is likely to be useful for you. Similarly, if you find yourself irritable, tense, and apprehensive a lot of the time, or if you have a nervous stomach, headaches, or nausea, associated with stress, then this program is likely to be useful for you.

Case Studies—Do You Relate?

To help you evaluate whether this program is suitable for you, read the following examples of people who were treated at our clinic for GAD.

Anne

Anne was a 38-year-old mother of two children, who were 12 and 14 years of age. She was a nurse, and was recently promoted to chief of her nursing unit. She had returned to nursing 6 years ago, after some time away from work while raising her children. Anne came to our clinic with complaints of excessive fatigue (tired all the time), irritability, headaches, and poor sleeping. On further questioning, it became apparent that Anne worried a great deal about managing her nursing unit, and she frequently became irritated and angry with the nurses she supervised for not devoting as much care to their duties as she thought they should. Therefore, she preferred to do many of the tasks herself, believing that it was her responsibility to make sure that everything was done in just the right way. In addition, Anne reported that she was frequently concerned about the future of her two children—not only their

2

current safety, but also how they would do in college and whether they would be happy when they got older. Finally, although she and her husband had no debts to speak of, Anne was continuously worried about whether they would have enough money to maintain their style of living, which was not overly indulgent, by any means.

Anne reported that she typically lay awake at night for an hour or two thinking of all of these things and of what she had to do the next day. When she was busy, such as dealing with a patient in distress or arguing with her family, her mind focused on the task at hand, and she didn't worry. However, whenever she was doing something routine, such as driving or household chores, her mind continually raced from one potential disaster to another. The disastrous images included being fired for not getting her work done and finding that her children were involved in a car accident. She continuously worried about the things that she needed to do to prevent these terrible things from happening. Her family had told her that, in recent months, she had become especially touchy and irritable. Anne herself noted that, since her promotion, her level of stress and anxiety had increased, and she never had a moment to relax. Anne stated that she remembered a time when she did not feel this way. She said that things did not worry her when she was in college the way they worried her now. It was not until the birth of her first child that she noticed herself taking everything so seriously, feeling as if she had to be prepared for any possibility of things going wrong, and worrying nearly every day.

James

James attended our clinic because he had generalized anxiety. He was a single, 35-year-old computer consultant and also was the co-owner of a bed and breakfast inn. James stated that he could not stop worrying about the future of the inn, and he became especially irritated with his business partner, who did not seem to be as worried about it. Little things around the inn, such as the way the towels were laid out on the beds or where the decorative items were placed, "bugged" James a great deal. He felt as if he could not sit still until everything was in its right place and perfect. In addition, he was very concerned with the financial status of the business, although it was doing very well and the rooms were occupied 90% of the time. In addition, James was always worried about making mistakes at work. He was concerned that he might be fired, despite the fact that his performance evaluations were satisfactory (and often complimentary), and no one had ever complained about his work.

As a result of his constant state of worry, James frequently experienced panic attacks. That is, he would experience a sudden rush of intense dread and very strong symptoms of shortness of breath and a racing heart that lasted only a short time. He understood that his high level of stress caused the panic attacks, and they were not a major concern for him. He was far more worried about his inn and his job than about panic attacks. In addition, James was very easily irritated by the smallest inconveniences, such as poor weather conditions that slowed the drive home after work and minor delays in receiving supply deliveries for the inn. His anger tended to interfere with his social relationships, since he frequently became irritated at the "stupidity" or "slowness" of others and felt that he could not rely on his friends and family to do things for him. In contrast to Anne, James reported that he had been a chronic worrier for as long as he could remember. Even in grade school, he recalled being worried about fitting in with the other kids and doing and saying the right things in class.

As these examples show, problems with generalized anxiety don't usually become so out of control that one can never get their tasks done. On the contrary, sometimes worriers use much more energy than they have to in completing unnecessary tasks, or completing tasks in an unreasonably short time (due to the sense of pressure from believing that everything has to be done immediately). On the other hand, worrying about possible negative outcomes can sometimes lead to procrastination and perfectionism. For example, you might "sit on" a report about the progress of a given project at work because of worries that it will be strongly criticized, and because of worries that you will be fired as a result. The most common impairment that results from generalized anxiety is a feeling that one isn't enjoying life, either because leisure activities are given up as one begins to think that there are too many other things to do or because the worry interferes with enjoying activities that once were pleasurable.

What Are the Specific Criteria for a Diagnosis of Generalized Anxiety Disorder?

To diagnose a person with GAD, mental health professionals use criteria set forth in the *Diagnostic and Statistical Manual of Mental Disorders,* published by the American Psychiatric Association (*DSM-IV;* APA, 1994).

In this disorder, the key feature is excessive and pervasive (or wide-ranging) worry about several life circumstances, such as relationships with family and friends, the health and well-being of oneself or one's family, home management and work responsibilities, finances, and self-worth, and various other concerns about neatness, being on time, and so on. Typically, the worry is focused on striving for perfection, avoiding making mistakes, maintaining a strong sense of responsibility, and attempting to maintain guardedness and control as a means of being prepared for and preventing bad things from happening. According to the *DSM-IV*, this type of worry must persist for at least six months and must not be the direct result of a real-life trauma, such as the kidnapping of one's child or a recent divorce. The *DSM-IV* also emphasizes the difficulty in stopping or "turning off" the worry, as would occur if you had difficulty going to sleep due to worrisome thoughts at bedtime. In addition, three or more of the symptoms shown in the following list must be present chronically for at least six months. These symptoms must not be the direct result of a physical disease or condition, such as menopause or a thyroid disorder. We recommend that our patients have a full medical examination to check for possible physical causes of anxiety symptoms (e.g., hyperthyroidism), especially if they have not had an examination within the last year.

Physical Symptoms of Generalized Anxiety Disorder (*Diagnostic and Statistical Manual of Mental Disorders*, 4th edition)

Restlessness or feeling keyed up or on edge

Being easily fatigued

Difficulty concentrating or mind going blank

Irritability

Muscle tension

Sleep disturbance (difficulty falling or staying asleep, or restless, unsatisfying sleep)

How Common Is This Problem?

Generalized anxiety is very common. The prevalence rate of GAD in the general population over the past year is estimated to be approximately 4%. In the United States, as many as 12 million people suffer from generalized anxiety. However, the experience of severe generalized anxiety is also an important part of most other anxiety and phobic disorders. In combination with other phobic and anxiety disorders, the percentage of the general population suffering from a disorder that involves generalized anxiety as a major component increases to approximately 10% to 12%. This represents a larger proportion of the general population than those who have alcohol or drug abuse problems, and makes anxiety disorders the number one mental health problem in the United States. All sorts of people, at all levels of socioeconomic status and in all professions, experience GAD.

Generalized Anxiety Disorder in the Elderly

Generalized anxiety disorder becomes more of a problem as we get older. In fact, GAD occurs less frequently in younger people, but increases dramatically with age, such that more than 7% of our elderly suffer from this condition. As we get older, our worry is more focused on health and safety, rather than work, family, and social functioning. For this reason, our elderly friends and relatives often think that they are less healthy than they really are, and that they should visit the doctor more often, or that they are in more danger of being harmed or of falling than they really are. While it is true that we are all at greater risk for falling and are less capable of defending ourselves as we get older, persons with GAD overestimate these risks.

Generalized Anxiety versus Life Crises

Many of the features described as characterizing GAD are similar to the symptoms experienced by people who have gone through a major life trauma. For example, most people who have lost a member of their family through a fatal car accident tend to worry and experience many of the physical symptoms listed earlier. The difference is that GAD does not depend on negative major life events, and in fact, the defining feature of the disorder is worrying when there is no real threat.

Another issue is the length of time that the worry and physical symptoms are experienced. If a traumatic event happens, and a year later, you are still worrying excessively about various life circumstances and still experiencing many of the physical symptoms of physical tension, it is likely that GAD has developed, perhaps triggered by the trauma. The worry and symptoms must be present for at least six months to be considered GAD.

Normal Worry versus Abnormal Worry

A question that naturally arises is how to distinguish between normal and abnormal worry. All of us tend to worry some of the time. Worry can serve a very adaptive function by helping us to prepare or problem-solve and decide how to cope with upcoming difficult situations (such as exams or work performance evaluations). When does worry become unadaptive, and why? We will be talking at length about the reasons that worry becomes excessive in the next chapter. One way to determine if your worry is "abnormal" is by asking yourself the following questions:

- Do you worry about things that you recognize that most people do not worry about (such as weeds in the garden)?

- Do you worry about things that others worry about (such as the safety of your children), but in a more exaggerated manner?

- Do you find it very difficult to stop worrying, and do you have trouble relaxing as a result?

- Do you worry much of the time without ever reaching a possible solution for a particular problem?

- Do you believe that, if you do not worry, a terrible event will actually happen?

- Do you worry about not being worried, or worry when everything is going well in your life?

- Do you believe that you will go crazy with worrying?

If you answer yes to most, or all, of these questions, you are probably experiencing more worry than is normal.

Worry in Other Emotional Disorders

Generalized anxiety is a feature of many types of anxiety and mood disorders. If you worry excessively and, at the same time, feel sad and hopeless, with a loss of interest and loss of energy (all of which are signs of a depressed mood), then consult with your mental health professional to learn if an alternative form of treatment is more appropriate than the treatment described here. Similarly, if your worry is restricted to a specific object (such as an animal), a specific situation (such as being stuck in an elevator or speaking in front of a large group), or a specific contaminant (such as certain chemicals that you avoid at all cost), seek the advice of a mental health professional as to whether this program will work for you. We have other programs in the Treatments That Work™ series that are suitable for specific phobias (*Mastery of Your Specific Phobia*), social anxiety (*Mastery of Your Social Anxiety*), and obsessions and compulsions (*Mastery of Your Obsessions and Compulsions*). If you are mostly worried about having panic attacks (sudden, and often unexpected, rushes of intense fear), then a program called *Mastery of Your Anxiety and Panic* may be more appropriate.

Is This Program Right for You?

The following list will help you to determine whether you can benefit from this program.

Have you:

- worried excessively and pervasively about several life circumstances (such as interpersonal relations, family, health, work, finances, or minor matters, such as chores or punctuality)?

- experienced difficulty controlling the worry?

- experienced at least some of the following physical symptoms throughout the day: restlessness or feeling keyed up, tiredness, difficulty concentrating, irritability, muscle tension, and sleep disturbance?

- experienced worry and physical "nervousness," for at least six months, for more days of the week than not?

- tended to worry and be physically tense, even when major life crises have not occurred?

- experienced physical symptoms that a medical doctor cannot attribute directly to physical or organic causes?

- noticed that your major problem revolves around chronic and uncontrollable worry about future events, instead of fear of specific objects, fear of social evaluation, fear of contamination, self-doubt, or fear of having panic attacks?

In this program, you will learn to control your "out-of-control" and un-productive worry and anxiety. The program is divided into twelve components, or chapters. In each chapter, you will learn specific skills. The skills will build on each other, so that in each new chapter, you will use skills learned in earlier chapters. The types of skills that you will learn include reducing physical tension, controlling excessive worry, and dealing with real problem situations. The program is obviously structured, but within that structure, there is room for individual tailoring.

At the end of each chapter, you will find homework and a self-assessment quiz that will help you to determine whether you've learned and retained the information in the chapter. If not, it is a sign for you to review the material again. Most people go over the chapters repeatedly. When you believe that you understand the material and have completed the exercises, you may go on to the next chapter. The importance of the exercises cannot be emphasized enough, because the success of the program is based largely on your completing them.

The pacing of the program is somewhat up to you. The most important issue is to complete the homework thoroughly and to understand the main points of each chapter before you begin the next chapter. The basic outline of the chapters is as follows:

Mastery of Your Anxiety and Worry Treatment Program Outline

1. Is this program right for you? The nature of generalized anxiety

2. Learning to recognize your own anxiety

3. The purpose and function of anxiety

4. A closer look at generalized anxiety disorder

5. Learning to relax

6. Controlling thoughts that cause anxiety: I. Overestimating the risk

7. Controlling thoughts that cause anxiety: II. Thinking the worst

8. Getting to the heart of worrying: Facing your fears

9. From fears to behaviors

10. Dealing with real problems: Time management, goal-setting, and problem-solving

11. Drugs for anxiety and their relation to this program

12. Your accomplishments and your future

Alternative Treatments

Even though you may have had contact with other mental health professionals in the past, or may have used drugs to treat your anxiety, you may still benefit from this program. However, some consideration must be given to other kinds of treatment that may be ongoing while you are participating in this program.

We recommend that, if you undertake this program, you should not be participating in other forms of psychotherapy that are also focused specifically on the treatment of anxiety. As with all treatments or programs that are focused on the same problem, messages can become mixed or confused. For that reason, we find it much more effective to do only one treatment program at a time. However, if you are participating in another psychotherapy program that is very general in its orientation or is focused on a very different area (for example, marital problems), then there is no reason why the two cannot be done at the same time.

If you are involved in another program right now that deals specifically with the treatment of generalized anxiety, we recommend that you continue with that program until you are sure that either it is effective (in which case you won't need another type of treatment) or it is ineffective (in which case you can try this program). As you will soon see, the type of program described in this workbook has been found to be very effective for many people, but that does not mean that other programs should not be given a fair trial. Different forms of therapy are more or less effective for different people. You must make this decision before you commit to go ahead with the program in this workbook.

This program will be appropriate even if you are currently taking drugs to control your anxiety. Many people enter our treatments while taking drugs. After finishing the treatment, approximately 50% of the people who were taking drugs, such as minor tranquilizers, stopped needing them and stopped taking them. Others stopped taking their medication with the help of their physician. Drugs used to treat anxiety will be described in more detail in chapter 11.

Ideally, you will be working on this program with the help of your doctor or a mental health professional, who may have given you this workbook.

What Benefits Will You Receive from This Program?

We developed this program at the Center for Stress and Anxiety Disorders, in Albany, New York. It has been substantially revised and updated at our Centers at Boston University (directed by Dr. Barlow) and the University of California at Los Angeles (directed by Dr. Craske). One of the purposes of our Centers is to develop new treatments for anxiety disorders. The National Institutes of Health and other funding agencies provide financial support, and our Centers have become well known for this activity, with the Boston Center being the largest clinical research facility of its kind in the world. From research studies conducted at our Centers, we have found that the type of treatment described in this program is quite successful. Approximately 70% of the people who complete the program are markedly improved, in terms of their physical symptoms, their tendency to worry, and the extent to which they generally find enjoyment in their daily lives. Furthermore, individuals tend to maintain their gains over the long term.

As with many of our programs designed to treat anxiety problems, one of the biggest predictors of successful outcome is the amount of practice that one does. The treatment is essentially a learning program, and it requires quite a bit of work and dedication. To help you decide if this treatment is right for you, think of all of the reasons why you want to make changes. Think of all of the times you feel exhausted and unhappy, the times you are irritable with your family and friends, and think of your own physical health. Then think of ways in which your life will be better when you learn to control your worry and anxiety.

What Is the Cost?

On the other side of the equation is the amount of time and energy needed to carry out this program over the next 10 to 12 weeks. The more you put into it, the more you will get out of it. We will be teaching you new ways of thinking and acting, but these changes have to come from you. These skills are only as good as the dedication of the person using them. With endurance and effort, these skills can be highly effective. It is not the severity of your anxiety, your age, or the length of time you have been a chronic worrier that determines success. Your motivation and persistence in making changes will determine your success. This is a decision for you to make right now, in light of the potential benefits. Do you have the motivation at this time to give this program your best effort? Remember that you are probably putting out as much energy and effort worrying and feeling anxious as you would be by going through this program, but with this program, positive changes will result. Also, remember that you cannot judge your success with a treatment accurately until you have given the treatment a fair trial. In other words, even if you have strong doubts about this particular treatment approach, wait until you have tried it to make a judgment.

If you do not have the motivation right now, then it is better to wait for another time. You will be defeating yourself by beginning a program like this halfheartedly. The following decision tree is designed to help you reach your final decision about whether to try this treatment now or to wait until you feel ready.

Decision Tree

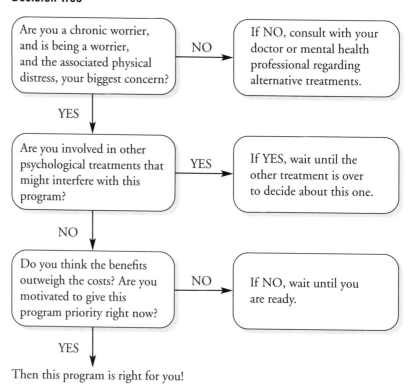

Chapter 2   *Learning to Recognize Your Own Anxiety*

Goals

- To learn the importance of record-keeping

- To introduce you to the Worry Record, Daily Mood Record, and Progress Record

- To learn how to monitor your anxiety for one week

- To complete the self-assessment

Record-Keeping

This chapter presents the importance of record-keeping and describes the method used in this program. For the rest of the time that you participate in this program, you must keep ongoing records of your mood state, among other things. Record-keeping is a necessary part of the success of this program.

Why Take the Time to Record? I Know I Am Anxious!

There are many reasons why it is important to keep records of your anxiety on a regular, ongoing basis. First, intense or chronic anxiety typically feels as if it is out of control or has a life of its own. You probably feel as if you are a victim of your own anxiety. Learning to be an observer, as opposed to a victim, of your own anxiety is a first step toward gaining control. Through record-keeping, you will learn to observe when, where, and under what circumstances your anxiety occurs. As a result, you will gain an understanding of the factors that cause your anxiety to increase and to continue, which in turn, will make you feel more in control and less of a victim.

Second, you will learn to understand the way in which you experience anxiety, in terms of what you think, what you feel, and what you do. This is very important because the treatment in this program is designed specifically to change anxious thinking, anxious feelings, and anxious behaviors. They cannot be changed without knowing exactly what they are.

Another important reason for regular, ongoing record-keeping is that this type of monitoring provides much more accurate information than you get by simply asking yourself, "How have I been feeling lately?" If you were asked to describe the last week, you may judge it to have been very bad, when in fact, there may have been several times when you felt relatively calm. When anxiety is on your mind so much, it is easy to forget about the times when you were not anxious. As you can probably see, thinking about the previous week as very "bad," while overlooking relatively "OK" times during the week, is likely to make you feel worse and more anxious. In fact, such negative judgments about how you've been doing in general may contribute to ongoing chronic anxiety. By keeping ongoing records, you will feel more in control and less anxious. Record-keeping forces you to recognize that your mood state fluctuates and that there are times when you feel less anxious than at other times.

Sometimes, people are concerned that, by continually recording their levels of anxiety, they will be reminded of how anxious they feel, which in turn, will make them feel even more anxious. You may be particularly concerned about this possible inflation effect if you are anxious or worried about feeling anxious (in other words if the anxiety feels as if it is out of your control). To address this concern, it is important to distinguish between two ways of monitoring mood states: subjective monitoring and objective monitoring.

Subjective monitoring means monitoring "how bad you feel," how severe the anxiety is, how much it interferes with your life, or how you can't control it. It's like being in the middle of a giant bowl of gelatin and feeling as if there's no way you can get out. Subjective monitoring is likely to be something that you already do, and maybe something that you try to avoid because it worsens your overall anxiety. Objective monitoring, which is the technique you will be learning in this chapter, means monitoring the features of anxiety in a more "scientific" way. You will learn to record things such as the number or intensity of symptoms, the triggers of your anxiety, and your thoughts and behavioral responses to anxiety. Objective monitoring is more like standing outside of the giant bowl of gelatin and noting exactly what color it is and how many times it shakes.

At first, it may be difficult to switch from subjective to objective monitoring, and as you start to use the records, you may indeed notice an increase in your anxiety because you are focusing on your feelings in the old, subjective way. However, with practice, most people are able to shift to the objective mode. To help you do this, we have developed very specific forms on which very specific objective information is to be recorded. These will be described soon.

Let's review all of the benefits of ongoing monitoring, as well as the reasons why it is crucial to this program:

- To identify specific triggers of episodes of high anxiety. Knowledge of these triggers and situations will lessen the sense of your anxiety being out of your control. It is easy to lose track of the specific triggers, partly because they can be very subtle and hard to identify, and partly because you may start to respond to triggers out of habit, without even knowing consciously what it is you are responding to. Record-keeping will help you to identify the triggers of your anxiety.

- To identify the specific ways in which you experience anxiety. These include your physical feelings, thoughts, and behaviors.

- To evaluate the success of your attempts to change. Remember, when you are anxious, it is easy to dismiss gains and focus instead on how anxious and terrible you feel. Objective monitoring will help you to appreciate your gains. When an episode of high anxiety makes you feel as if you've failed or fallen back, the records will show the changes that you've made, so that the one incident of high anxiety does not overshadow your progress. So, keep all of your forms for the purpose of review. It's a good idea to start a folder for your records.

- To become an objective observer of yourself so that you can begin to stand outside the bowl of gelatin. This is an important step in your progress.

What Do I Record?

The various procedures that you will be taught in the following chapters will have their own forms that will be explained to you with each chapter. However, there are two records that you are asked to use for the entire program.

The first form is called a Worry Record. This form is to be used any time that you notice a sharp increase in your anxiety, when you find yourself worrying, or when you're experiencing particular physical symptoms, such as irritability, muscle tension, poor concentration, restlessness, or feeling keyed up, or increased fatigue or sleep disturbance. Information from this particular monitoring form will be invaluable for understanding the triggers and components of your anxiety.

The form has eight sets of ratings. At the top, record the date and the time that the episode of heightened anxiety began. Next, circle the maximum level of anxiety that you felt, from the time that you noticed the anxiety episode had begun until now (the time that you are completing the form). Then, check any of the symptoms that you experienced, from the time that the episode began until now. Although you may feel some of these symptoms "all the time," indicate which ones you felt more intensely than usual. Then, give a brief description of the triggers that may have contributed to your heightened anxiety. These triggers might include the time of day (such as just before the end of the workday, when you start to worry about not having enough time to get everything done), reading a newspaper article about diseases, failing to hear from a family member at an expected time, and so on. If you don't know what triggered your anxiety, just write "don't know." Then, in the "Anxious thoughts" section, record what you are worried about happening. This part of the record is very important, so be as specific as you can in describing your thoughts. We will spend a lot of time on the nature of anxious thoughts in chapter 3. Next, record your behaviors in response to your worry, such as pacing, calling to check on family members, or trying to distract your mind from worrying. Finally, record at what time you noticed a marked decrease in your worry or a decline in the intensity of your physical sensations (at the top right corner of the Worry Record). A blank copy of the Worry Record is shown. (Note: Two different versions of the Worry Record will be used once you get to chapters 6 and 7.)

As can be seen from the following example, James became very anxious at around 5 P.M. Sunday, and reported that he felt that way for the next four hours. His maximum level of anxiety by the time he made his ratings was 60, or strong. He noted restlessness and feeling keyed up, difficulty concentrating, and irritability. He was unable to relate his anxiety to any specific triggering event, except that it was the night before the beginning of a new workweek, and he typically became quite anxious on Sunday nights, when thinking of the coming week. James noted that he was thinking about

Worry Record

Date: _____ Time began: _____ (A.M./P.M.) Time ended: _____ (A.M./P.M.)

Maximum level of anxiety (circle a number below):

0 ----- 10 ----- 20 ----- 30 ----- 40 ----- 50 ----- 60 ----- 70 ----- 80 ----- 90 ----- 100

   None   Mild   Moderate   Strong   Extreme

Indicate which of the following symptoms you are experiencing:

Restlessness, feeling keyed up or on edge _____

Easily fatigued _____

Difficulty concentrating or mind going blank _____

Irritability _____

Muscle tension _____

Sleep disturbance _____

Triggering events: _____

_____

_____

Anxious thoughts: _____

_____

_____

Anxious behaviors: _____

_____

_____

Worry Record for James

Date: _Sunday 9th_   Time began: _5:00_   (A.M. (P.M.))   Time ended: _9:00_   (A.M. (P.M.))

Maximum level of anxiety (circle a number below):

0 ----- 10 ----- 20 ----- 30 ----- 40 ----- 50 ---(60)--- 70 ----- 80 ----- 90 ----- 100

    None   Mild   Moderate   Strong   Extreme

Indicate which of the following symptoms you are experiencing:

Restlessness, feeling keyed up or on edge	✓
Easily fatigued	_____
Difficulty concentrating or mind going blank	✓
Irritability	✓
Muscle tension	_____
Sleep disturbance	_____

Triggering events: _Sunday night—work tomorrow_

Anxious thoughts: _Too much to do, won't get everything finished, boss will be mad at me_

Anxious behaviors: _Tried to watch TV to keep my mind occupied, but I continued to worry_

all of the problems that could occur at work and how they would interfere with the tight schedule he had that week. He said that he worried about not getting everything done in time and being criticized by his boss. His anxious behaviors included attempted distraction by watching TV, but he was unsuccessful.

In the next example, Anne reported that she felt very anxious (a maximum of 70) on Thursday at 2.00 P.M. She felt restlessness, difficulty concentrating, and muscle tension. The triggering event that she noted was that her husband did not call at his usual time. Anne noted that she was worried

Worry Record for Ann

Date: _Thursday 15th_   Time began: _2:00_ (A.M. / **P.M.**) Time ended: _2:45_ (A.M. / **P.M.**)

Maximum level of anxiety (circle a number below):

0 ----- 10 ----- 20 ----- 30 ----- 40 ----- 50 ----- 60 ---（70）--- 80 ----- 90 ----- 100

   None   Mild   Moderate   Strong   Extreme

Indicate which of the following symptoms you are experiencing:

Restlessness, feeling keyed up or on edge   ___✓___

Easily fatigued   _____

Difficulty concentrating or mind going blank   ___✓___

Irritability   _____

Muscle tension   ___✓___

Sleep disturbance   _____

Triggering events: _Mark did not call me when he was supposed to_

Anxious thoughts: _Maybe he is sick, his stomach problems could have developed into something serious, he collapsed_

Anxious behaviors: _Kept calling Mark on his cell phone—called at least 10 times_

about his safety (and continued worrying until he called 45 minutes later). In particular, she was worried that his recent stomach complaints could have turned into a major physical problem, and she imagined him collapsing at work. Consequently, her behavioral response was to repeatedly try to call her husband on his cell phone.

The information that you record on these forms will help you to understand patterns in your anxiety response that you may not have been aware of before.

Daily Mood Record

Rate each column at the end of the day, using a number from the 0- to 100-point scale below.

0 ----- 10 ----- 20 ----- 30 ----- 40 ----- 50 ----- 60 ----- 70 ----- 80 ----- 90 ----- 100

None   Mild   Moderate   Strong   Extreme

Date	Overall Anxiety	Maximum Anxiety	Overall Physical Tension	Overall Preoccupation with Worry	

The second form is the Daily Mood Record, to be completed at the end of each day, just before you go to sleep.

We find it most helpful to use a scale of 0 to 100 points for rating levels of anxiety. In the first column, record your average, or overall, level of anxiety over the day, by taking all of the day into consideration. Choose a number from 0 to 100, where 100 equals extreme anxiety and 0 equals no anxiety. These 0- to 100-point ratings will become second nature to you after a little practice. Using a number scale is a much more objective method of rating your mood state than recording words or phrases about how you feel. In the second column, record the maximum, or highest, level of anxiety you felt during the day, using the same 0- 100-point scale. If nothing important happened during the day and you did not experience episodes of heightened anxiety, then the numbers in the first two columns should be the same. In the third column, record your average or overall level of physical tension or discomfort, including aches and pains, irritability, poor concentration, restlessness, fatigue, and difficulty sleeping, taking all of the day into consideration. In the fourth column, record your average or overall level of preoccupation with worries, again taking all of the day into consideration, in other words, how much of the day your mind was focused on worrisome thoughts. The fifth column is left blank in case you have something specific that you want to additionally monitor (such as procrastination or nail biting).

In the following example, we can see that James had a mixed week, with some days having higher ratings than other days. Remember, if we had asked James at the end of the week how this week had been, he may have said that he was anxious all week, when in fact, his anxiety level, physical ten-

Daily Mood Record for James

Rate each column at the end of the day, using a number from the 0- to 100-point scale below.

0 ----- 10 ----- 20 ----- 30 ----- 40 ----- 50 ----- 60 ----- 70 ----- 80 ----- 90 ----- 100

| | None | Mild | Moderate | Strong | Extreme |

Date	Overall Anxiety	Maximum Anxiety	Overall Physical Tension	Overall Preoccupation with Worry	Headaches
Monday 7th	45	85	65	75	50
Tuesday 8th	25	50	45	45	10
Wednesday 9th	60	90	70	70	65
Thursday 10th	15	25	20	25	10
Friday 11th	40	60	50	55	30
Saturday 12th	25	30	10	30	15
Sunday 13th	50	50	30	40	20

sion, and preoccupation with worry were quite mild on two days (Tuesday and Thursday). James elected to rate headaches as well, because they were a particularly frequent and distressing symptom for him.

Finally, it is important to keep a chart of your improvement, based on information gathered from the Worry Record and the Daily Mood Record. The Progress Record is designed to summarize your progress over the week so that you can easily view changes over the course of the entire program. You can select any feature that you are recording to summarize on your Progress Record. A blank copy of the Progress Record follows. At the very least, we recommend that you record the number of anxiety episodes that you ex-

Progress Record

Left axis: Number of anxiety episodes per week (from the number of Worry Records)

Right axis: Average of daily maximum anxiety per week (from the Daily Mood Record)

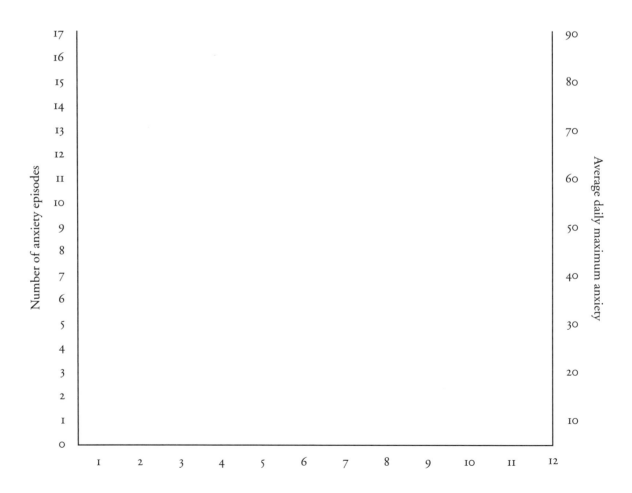

perience each week (determined from the number of Worry Records that you complete each week) and the average of the maximum anxiety ratings that you make over the course of a week. To determine the maximum anxiety rating average, simply average all of the 0- to 100-point ratings that you record under the "Maximum Anxiety" column on the Daily Mood Record for one week.

As shown in the following example, James completed 12 Worry Records during his first week, and on his Daily Mood Record, he had the following maximum anxiety ratings: 70, 60, 30, 70, 30, 40, 50. First he added these ratings to get a total (in his case, it equals 350). Then, he divided his total by

Progress Record for James

Left axis: Number of anxiety episodes per week (from the number of Worry Records)

Right axis: Average of daily maximum anxiety per week (from the Daily Mood Record)

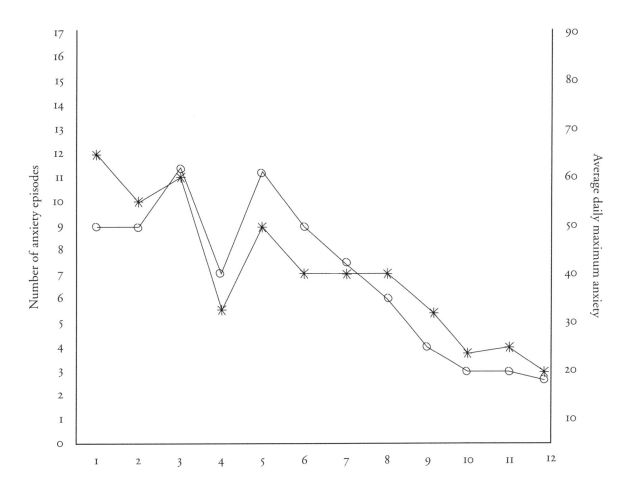

the number of ratings (350 divided by 70, in this example) to get his maximum anxiety average of 50 for the first week. During the second week, he completed 10 Worry Records, and the average of his maximum anxiety was 50. You can see how the remainder of the weeks turned out.

The Progress Record is divided into weeks, up to 12 weeks, but you can add more, if necessary. This graph will help you to keep everything in perspective. It may be helpful to place the Progress Record in a very visible place, such as on your bathroom mirror or refrigerator (or somewhere where it is not visible to others, but very noticeable to you), so that you will be reminded of the positive changes that you are making.

One cannot emphasize enough the importance of this record-keeping. The Worry Record and the Daily Mood Record must be completed daily to get the full benefit of the program. At first, you may have to push yourself to keep these records, but it will become easier, and even rewarding, as you continue. It helps to give yourself feedback, and the information is also very helpful to your mental health professional.

Homework

✎ Begin to monitor your anxiety episodes and daily anxiety for a full week, using the Worry Record and Daily Mood Record.

Self-Assessment

Answer each of the following questions by circling T (true) or F (false). Answers are given in the appendix.

1. Recording your anxiety daily or as it happens is more accurate and more objective than recalling your anxiety over the past week.   T   F

2. It is best to fill in the Worry Record at the end of the week so that you are not continually thinking about how anxious you feel.   T   F

3. Daily recording helps you to identify specific situations and triggers for your anxiety episodes.   T   F

Chapter 3   *The Purpose and Function of Anxiety*

Goals

▪ To review your records from the previous week and add data to your Progress Record

▪ To understand both the purpose of anxiety and its components

▪ To recognize your own physical symptoms of anxiety and record them

▪ To fill out the Sequence of Anxiety Components form

▪ To continue record-keeping

▪ To complete the self-assessment

Review of Your Records

Did you complete your ongoing monitoring using the Worry Record for each episode of heightened anxiety as well as the Daily Mood rating? If you did not do the record-keeping, think of ways to improve your compliance, because this program depends on accurate record-keeping. In fact, record-keeping is the first step toward change. As explained in the previous chapter, record-keeping enables you to develop a more objective level of self-awareness. Keeping objective records will help you to feel more in control of your anxiety and worry. In addition, the monitoring is essential for obtaining detailed information about the way in which you experience anxiety—what you physically feel, what you think, and what you do. If you have not completed any monitoring, we recommend that you use the following week to monitor before continuing with the program.

If you have completed the monitoring, well done! Now, look at your records to see what you can learn. Does your anxiety occur in response to the same types of triggers time after time, such as work responsibilities or family events? Do the same types of thoughts tend to come to mind when you are anxious, or are they varied? What time of day or day of the week do you experience the most anxiety? It may be too early to detect patterns, or it may not. Also, now that you have kept a full week of records, the summary can be added to the Progress Record. Fill in the number of anxiety episodes that you experienced over the past week (by counting the number of Worry Records) and the average maximum anxiety rating (by averaging the maximum anxiety ratings you made each day on the Daily Mood form). Of course, you may add other summaries to your Progress Record as well.

Looking for patterns in the triggers and the way you experience anxiety is the first step toward learning that anxiety is a reaction. Although it may feel as if it is out of your control, anxiety is a reaction to something. There are ways of changing or learning to react differently, once you know what the triggers are. Let's examine the nature of anxiety and discuss specifically the process of worry—why it begins in the first place, and how it keeps going.

The State of Anxiety

Anxiety is a natural state that is experienced by everybody. In many cases, anxiety is a productive, driving force. Think of performers, who have to get up on stage in front of a large crowd; having some anxiety will motivate them to perform at their best. Years of research have shown over and over again that having some anxiety enhances performance: that is, you do better at what you're doing, whether in the classroom, at a business meeting, or on the tennis court, when anxiety rises to a certain optimal level.

Anxiety has one overriding purpose, and that is protection and preparation. Anxiety prepares you to deal with threats or dangers that could happen at any minute. When you think a threat or danger is about to occur, anxiety helps you to shift into a state of fearful fight or flight (the natural reaction to immediate danger). While anxiety is similar to fear, the two are somewhat different. Anxiety is the state of preparation for danger that could occur in the future. Fear is the response that occurs when the threat or danger is perceived as being immediately present. Anxiety makes the activation of fear easier. For instance, imagine that you are walking through a jungle and are concerned that a lion may be hiding behind the trees. You would be in a state of anxiety, and as a result, you would be on guard, watching for any signs of possible lion attack. Your body would be geared up and ready to take action, if necessary. If a lion suddenly emerged from the trees and ran toward you, the emotion of fear and the associated "fight-or-flight" response would take over so that you would either run away or face the danger. The bottom line is that fear and anxiety are protective.

When anxiety is chronic, however, it is as if you are in a state of constant preparation for threat or danger. Importantly, the threat does not have to be real, since anxiety can occur when you only think that danger or threat could happen. The danger or threat does not have to mean something as severe as your life being threatened by a killer. It can be anything that is negative, ranging from the threat of death to the threat of ridicule or failure. A successful business executive who is challenged by a new assignment or project may experience considerable stress and anxiety and may be driven to work long hours in order to avoid failure, criticism, and a sense of loss of mastery and control. Or, a mother of three children may be challenged by the demands of school and may become anxious that her children will fail. From this, it should be clear that different people find different things threatening or challenging.

Let's look at some examples. Suppose you are having a hard day at the office and you have a deadline to meet by 5:00 P.M. or your boss will be upset. Or, suppose your sister-in-law is picking you up in 15 minutes to go to a meeting. Your young children aren't cooperating, and you're not close to being ready. You know that your sister-in-law will be annoyed and that you'll be late for the meeting. Here, the threats are less obvious, but they are still present. You may fail to meet your deadline and be criticized by your boss, a person who is important to you, or you may upset your sister-in-law and interrupt a meeting by entering after it has begun. If you did not care at all about the task at work or the meeting, or about the reaction of your boss or your sister-in-law, you would most likely feel no anxiety.

In these examples, the deadlines and timelines clearly are the immediate triggers for anxiety. As we mentioned earlier, many times, it is unclear what is triggering anxiety, and one of the first goals of this program is to discover those triggers.

Continuing with our examples, if the anxiety were severe enough, and you became convinced that the worst you imagined was about to come true (that you would be fired or that your children would be harmed, for example), you might experience the fearful fight-or-flight response right in your office or at home. This fear response would occur, even though there was no real, immediate danger. You might experience a panic attack and feel as if you were losing control, having a heart attack, or suffocating. Then, you would feel like escaping or "getting out," even though you knew there was really nothing to be afraid of. On the other hand, you might experience the "fight" response, lash out, and slap your kids, or lose your temper with the workers in your office, almost before you realized it was happening.

Now that the nature of anxiety has been described, it is important to recognize that, although it is a natural response when threat is perceived, anxiety becomes problematic if it is experienced too frequently or too intensely. Anxiety can vary tremendously in severity, from mild uneasiness to extreme distress, and it can vary in frequency, from occasional to seemingly constant unease. When anxiety is very intense or very frequent, it can interfere with your life and feel as if it is out of control. The goal of this program is to help you learn to reduce the frequency or intensity of your anxiety, but not to remove anxiety altogether, because that would be not only impossible, but also undesirable. A little anxiety is needed to motivate performance, and a lot of anxiety is needed when there are real threats.

Components of Anxiety

Anxiety is difficult to manage when viewed as a whole, since the global approach does not provide clues for controlling anxiety. How many times have you said to yourself (or heard others say to you), "Just calm down. Stop being so anxious." How many times has that statement been effective in calming you? It probably hasn't worked very well because telling yourself to be less anxious does not tell you *how* to do it. Thinking about anxiety in terms of its components takes away a lot of its mystery and its seemingly uncontrollable quality. In addition, thinking about anxiety in terms of its parts helps you to identify ways to learn to be less anxious. Scientists often break anxiety down into three components: physical, cognitive (thoughts), and behavioral. That is why you have begun to record your physical symptoms, your thoughts, and your behaviors. Let's spend some time understanding these different components.

Physical Component

The physical component involves physical sensations or symptoms, such as muscular tension, irritability, fatigue, restlessness, and difficulty concentrating. The nervous system causes various physical effects during states of anxiety and fear, and since some of the symptoms seem unexplainable or unusual (such as blurry vision or pressure in your head), they can also provoke anxiety. However, remember that the physical symptoms are the side effects of a response that is meant to protect you as your body prepares for danger or threat. Although the symptoms may seem frightening, they are actually part of a self-protective system and are not dangerous at all.

When danger or threat is perceived, the brain sends messages to a section of your nerves called the "autonomic nervous system." The autonomic nervous system has two branches, called the "sympathetic nervous system" and the "parasympathetic nervous system." These two branches of the nervous system are directly involved in controlling the body's energy levels when preparing for action. Simply put, the sympathetic nervous system is the one that prepares the body for threat or danger by making it ready for the fight-or-flight response: it primes the body for action. The parasympathetic system is responsible for regaining balance and restoring the system to a normal resting state. However, these two systems do not always work in unison. A useful analogy is the accelerator (representing the sympathetic nervous system) and brake (representing the parasympathetic nervous system) pedals in a car; at any given second, only the accelerator, only the brakes, both the accelerator and the brakes, or neither may be in use.

Recent research indicates that chronic worry and anxiety are associated more with low levels of parasympathetic activity than with high levels of sympathetic arousal. Low levels of parasympathetic control mean that the brakes are used less of the time; the accelerator may not be in full throttle, but nonetheless, it is not being controlled by the brakes as well as it could be. The result is a sustained physiological response, without a lot of change. This may explain the chronic symptoms of GAD, such as muscle tension, backache, headache, poor sleep, irritability, and difficulty relaxing. In contrast, the physiology associated with specific fears leads to physical symptoms that increase quickly and then decrease in the presence and absence, respectively, of the anxiety-producing object.

Fortunately, some of our own research has shown that low levels of parasympathetic activation can be corrected with the type of treatment that is described in this workbook.

In contrast to chronic worry and anxiety is the physiology of fear, which is brought on by a perceived immediate threat. Under such conditions, the sympathetic nervous system takes charge and releases two chemicals from the adrenal glands of the kidney. These chemicals are called "adrenaline" and "noradrenaline." They are used as messengers by the sympathetic nervous system to tell the rest of the body to prepare for fight or flight. Other chemicals in the body eventually destroy adrenaline and noradrenaline, so the fight-or-flight arousal cannot continue forever, although the response may continue to rise and fall, and even after the immediate danger and the surge of emotion have passed, you are likely to feel keyed up for some time. This is perfectly natural. In fact, this prolonged response has an adaptive function, because in the wild, danger has a habit of returning, and it is useful for the organism to remain in a prepared state to reactivate the emergency response (fear), if necessary.

The chemical changes that activate the fight-or-flight response produce various symptoms. For example, the heart rate increases, which helps to speed up blood flow, thus improving the delivery of oxygen to and removal of waste products from the tissues. When this occurs, it is common to feel as if your heart is racing or pounding very hard. There is also a change in blood flow. Basically, blood is redirected away from the places where it is not needed, such as the skin, fingers, and toes, and toward the places where it is needed, such as the large muscles in the arms, legs, and chest, by an expansion and constriction of the different blood vessels. When this occurs, it is common to feel your feet and hands becoming cold, and even numb or tingly. In addition, breathing usually becomes faster. This has obvious importance for the body's self-defense, since the tissues need to get more oxygen so that you can move more quickly. In turn, you might feel breathless, a sensation of being smothered, or discomfort, or even pain, in your chest. One side effect of an increased breathing rate and hyperventilation (when the oxygen is not actually consumed at the rate at which it is taken in) is that the blood supply to the brain is actually reduced. While it is only slightly reduced and is not dangerous, it produces a collection of unpleasant symptoms, including dizziness, blurred vision, confusion, a feeling of unreality, and perhaps a sensation of not getting enough air. Usually, sweat gland activity also increases, as a way of cooling the body and preventing overheating, should you have to fight or flee.

Various other physical changes take place during fear, or the fight-or-flight response, including widening of the pupils, which might result in various strange visual effects (such as increased intensity of visual stimulation or blurred vision). A decrease in salivation also occurs, causing dry mouth, as well as a decrease in activity in the digestive system, which often produces a heavy feeling in the stomach.

As you can see, whereas the physiology of worry and chronic anxiety (about future uncertain or threatening events) involves chronically elevated muscle tension and restlessness, with little change, the physiology of fear (when one feels immediately threatened) is associated with a distinct peak in sympathetic nervous system arousal. You might feel the physical effects of chronic anxiety most of the time and feel the effects of fear occasionally, especially at those moments when you become convinced that what you are most worried about is actually going to come true. This distinction between anxiety and fear is important because the state of anxiety and worry may actually block the physiological experience of fear. In other words, worrying may block the physiological reactions associated with being afraid. As described later, it may even be the case that worry will continue because it feels better than being afraid. For example, feeling tense and irritable, with difficulty sleeping, is better than feeling short of breath, dizzy, or disoriented, with your heart racing. In this way, anxiety and worry may become a way of avoiding fear. One of the goals of this program is to learn to face the fear, so that it has a chance to subside, and thereby lessen the need for worry.

Thinking Component

Similar to the body's preparation for a threat or danger, the mind also prepares, when in an anxious state. One of the major effects of feeling anxious is a shift of attention toward the source of threat. Thoughts or images become focused on a sense of impending doom, thoughts that something bad is about to happen, or nervous wondering about what is going to happen. There is usually a tendency to believe that negative events are particularly likely to happen, even though their actual probability is very low. There is also a tendency to focus exclusively on the worst possible outcome, instead of the more positive outcomes.

When we feel anxiety, our minds naturally scan our environment for possible signs of threat. This is valuable in terms of survival, because it means that you will notice danger very quickly, if it does exist. However, if you are chronically anxious, your persistent focus on the possibility of a threat, or of things going wrong in the future, is likely to interfere with your attention to things going on right in front of you, such as the conversations happening at the moment or your current job tasks. You are more likely to be distracted.

Anxious thoughts (the ones that have to do with all of the possible negative outcomes) are referred to as "worry," which is a main feature of GAD. We will spend some time discussing the role of worry. At this point, it is important for you to recognize that anxious thoughts or images are one component of your anxiety. In addition, worrisome thoughts can contribute to other components of anxiety (such as the physiology and behaviors), and the physiology and behaviors of anxiety can also contribute to worrisome thoughts. The interactions among thoughts, behaviors, and physiology are described in more detail later in this chapter.

There are a number of common themes in chronic worry:

1. *Health.* This can include worries about your own health or the health of family and friends, images of sickness and disease, and your own inability to cope, should you or somebody close to you become sick. You may become anxious when hearing about others falling ill because it reminds you of the possibility that you or a loved one might become sick.

2. *Friends/family.* This can include worries about being a good parent or friend, the general happiness and well-being of your family and friends, their safety, and whether you are saying or doing the right things by them.

3. *Work/school.* This is another area that is often a source of worry. For example, you might worry about completing all of the tasks for the day or the week, wonder whether you are performing at the level that is expected or making mistakes, or wonder whether the entire office for which you are responsible is working in the way that it should.

4. *Finances.* Sometimes people worry about paying their bills or having enough money for the future, even though they do have enough money to cover their expenses.

5. *Daily life.* These worries include thinking that a negative outcome is lurking around every corner, including constant worry about day-to-day activities, such as being on time, traffic, presenting a good appearance, chores, and so on.

Although people who are chronic worriers tend to worry about the same kinds of things as people who are not chronic worriers, chronic worry is characterized by an added dimension of not being able to stop the worry. The chronic worrier may lie in bed at night, worrying about upcoming events during the week or the years to come, despite the desire to stop worrying, whereas others are more easily able to dismiss their worries. Similarly, the chronic worrier may bring work-related worries home, instead of being able to "turn them off." A good deal of this program is aimed at helping you to learn how to "turn off" worries.

Several underlying beliefs are associated with chronic worry; and these beliefs may explain, in large part, why it is so difficult to turn off the worry.

1. *Perfectionism,* or the underlying belief that one cannot, and should not, make mistakes, and that to make mistakes, in judgment, decision-making, parenting, work, or wherever, represents incompetence in managing life.

2. *Responsibility,* or the underlying belief that it is irresponsible not to attend to negative possibilities, that worries that pop up in one's mind should not be ignored, and that worrying means that you are being responsible, whereas not worrying is to be irresponsible.

3. *Controllability,* or the underlying belief that worry is a way of gaining control and preventing negative possibilities from coming true. In other words, "I am glad I worried about my daughter because she made it home safely from her trip," or conversely, "I am worried that I am not worrying."

4. *Negative beliefs about worry,* or the belief that worry itself may drive you crazy, or that worrying indicates that you have lost your mind or are incapable of functioning.

These underlying beliefs either drive you to continue to worry (because worry means that "you are less likely to make mistakes," "that you are being responsible," and that "you are preventing negative events from coming true") or drive you to do things to stop yourself from worrying, such as distracting yourself or always being fully prepared for the next workday so that you won't have to worry throughout the night about not being fully prepared (because excessive worry during the night might "make you lose your mind"). Either way, these underlying beliefs perpetuate worry.

Behavioral Component

The thinking and physical state of being prepared for danger or a threat (anxiety) obviously has certain behavioral features that accompany it. Some of the behaviors are directly produced by high levels of physical tension. These include restlessness, poor concentration on other tasks, and irritability.

Other behaviors include those that are designed to lessen the amount of worrying, such as always being fully prepared for the next day at work so as to avoid worrying throughout the night about not being prepared, or refusing to take on a task to avoid worrying about its completion.

Other behaviors are designed to prevent the chances of negative outcomes, and of course, these overlap with the behaviors designed to prevent worry in the first place. For example, being overly prepared for the next day of work not only helps to eliminate worry about not being prepared, but also, in your mind, may help decrease the chances of being criticized at work the next day. The same applies to going overboard to ensure that everything gets done on time at work or at home. Similarly, working to have your house in perfect order before a social gathering at home serves not only to decrease your worry about the order of your house, but also, in your mind, decreases the chances of negative judgments from your guests.

Related to this are "safety-check" types of behaviors, designed to ensure that "everything is OK." These can include things such as calling your husband or wife at work each day to be reassured that he or she is safe, checking the news reports for weather conditions in the areas in which your family members are driving, and being overly protective of your children. Of course, these types of safety checks are common for a lot of people, but you may do them more frequently than others, and the immediate relief that they provide, unfortunately, contributes to anxiety.

As you will learn, all of the behaviors that are designed to eliminate worry or prevent negative events contribute to your chronic worry in the long run. We will help you let go of these behaviors.

Now that each of the components of anxiety has been described, it is time for you to recognize the physical symptoms, thoughts or images, and behaviors that occur when you are anxious. Remember, an initial step toward change is to become an objective observer of your own reactions. Using the Worry Records that you completed over the last week, list your most typical physical symptoms, thoughts, and behaviors. In the following example, when James is anxious, he is most aware of jittery legs, an upset stomach, and muscle tension. His thoughts are mostly related to making mistakes at work and losing his job, not getting everything at work done on time, and his future. His major behaviors include irritability with others at work and at home, procrastination about big tasks, and frequent reviews of his work.

Now, record the types of symptoms, thoughts, and behaviors that you most commonly experience when you are anxious and worried about future events or uncertainties. Use your record-keeping over the past week to help you. Remember, your physical symptoms, behaviors, and thoughts are likely to differ, depending on whether you are in a state of anxiety or a state of fear (the actual fight-or-flight response). For example, although you might feel jittery, tense, and irritable when you are worried about the future, the most noticeable symptoms when you are afraid might be a racing heart and un-

Anxiety Components for James

Major physical symptoms: _Jittery, tense legs_
knot in stomach
tension, especially head & neck

Major thoughts/images: _Errors at work, lose job_
Not getting things done
Future of family

Major behaviors: _Irritable with colleagues & family_
Procrastinate about starting big jobs
Review my work over and over

Anxiety Components

Major physical symptoms: _____

_____

_____

_____

Major thoughts/images: _____

_____

_____

_____

Major behaviors: _____

_____

_____

_____

steadiness or faintness. Similarly, when you are worried about the future, your behaviors might be to work extra hard to prevent negative events (such as being fired from your job), whereas you might just leave or escape a situation when you feel very frightened. Finally, the major thought when you are anxious is likely to pertain to possible future events ("what if") whereas your strongest thoughts when you are afraid are likely to relate to the perception of immediate danger ("It is happening. I am about to die"). For this particular exercise, write down the symptoms, thoughts, and behaviors that occur when you are anxious and worried about future events.

The Anxiety Component Cycle

The three components of anxiety not only define the experience of anxiety, but also influence each other in a way that can increase or decrease the overall experience of anxiety. Let's examine the escalating cycle first. At times, worrisome thoughts may bring about increased physical tension, which may, in turn, interfere with your behavior. For example, worrying about the safety of your friends or family may result in agitation and restlessness to a level that interferes with your concentration at work. In turn, high levels of physical tension most likely contribute to having worrisome thoughts or images. This type of interaction, where one component of anxiety intensifies another component, is called a "positive feedback loop." Another example of a positive feedback loop is when worrying about receiving a negative review at work produces increased muscle tension and difficulty concentrating, which produce more anxious thoughts about being fired, which contribute

The Anxiety Component Cycle

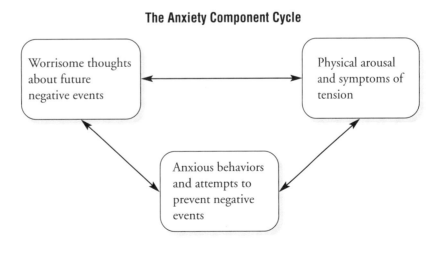

37

to even higher levels of physical tension and overwhelming fatigue, which lead to procrastination about starting a new project at work, which intensifies worries about being fired, and the cycle goes on. Therefore, while representing separate components, the thoughts, behaviors, and physiology can interact in ways that actually cause further anxiety, as shown.

Let's take another example. James was at his computer programming work one Friday morning, anxiously worrying about renovations that were being made at his bed and breakfast inn. His worry had been relatively mild, until he overheard a co-worker talking about problems he'd had with a plumber in his own home. The plumber did not show up on time, and as a result, the kitchen sink was still clogged and would remain so until the plumber returned that evening. When James heard this account, he began to worry that the renovations to his inn would not be completed by the evening. If that happened, it would be a disaster because the customers who were coming for the weekend would be disappointed with the condition of the inn. As he continued to worry, James began to feel tense and restless. He called the company responsible for the renovations, but the person in charge was out of the office. This led James to feel even more worried, and he became increasingly convinced that the workers had not shown up at all. He tried to focus on his work, but found it very difficult to stop thinking about the renovations, because he was very agitated and was experiencing some stomach distress. As a result, he began to worry about others noticing him at work. He worried that they would think that he was not getting his work done. This led to other worries about being fired from his job and being in the horrible position of not being able to pay the bills.

In fact, most of the renovations went according to plan, and even though every last detail was not finished, the customers still seemed very pleased with the inn. As usual, the result was very different from the images of disaster that James was preoccupied with while at work. In this case, a specific piece of information led to worrisome thoughts and images, as well as physical tension, safety checking behaviors, task interference, and so on. Therefore, a feedback cycle was operating, whereby negative thoughts provoked physical tension and behaviors, which provoked more negative thoughts, and so on.

Now it's time for you to describe one of your own recent episodes of anxiety in the same way. What was the sequence of events? Understanding your

Sequence of Anxiety Components for a Recent Episode of Anxiety

anxiety in this way will contribute to a sense of control; by understanding the patterns that cause anxiety to increase, it becomes possible to interrupt these patterns and gain control over your anxiety. Use the following form to record the sequence of thoughts, behaviors, and physical symptoms for a recent episode of anxiety, perhaps one that you have already recorded on a Worry Record. Note that, on the Worry Record, you recorded your thoughts, symptoms, and behaviors, whereas in the Sequence of Anxiety Components form, you are recording the way in which one anxiety component influenced another anxiety component in positive feedback loops.

Just as the cycle can escalate, it can also spiral downward. Learning to interrupt an escalating cycle and turn it into a downward cycle, so that unnecessary anxiety decreases, is the basic approach taken in this program. For example, let's go back to the example of James. When he first began to worry about the renovations, he felt physically tense. If he had reassured himself at that point that it was more likely than not that the renovations would be completed, and, even if they were not finished, it would not be the end of the world, a very different emotional experience would have resulted. Instead of further escalation, the physical tension probably would have decreased, and he would have returned to focusing on his tasks at work. Then, the worries related to being fired from his office job would not have popped up at all.

Homework

✎ Over the following week, pay special attention to how your worrisome thoughts and images intensify your physical tension and lead to anxious behaviors and further worry.

✎ For every episode of anxiety that you record on the Worry Record form, identify positive feedback loops among your anxiety components.

✎ Reread this chapter several times to ensure that you fully understand the concept of three components of anxiety.

✎ Continue record-keeping using the Worry Record and the Daily Mood Record.

Answer each of the following questions by circling T (true) or F (false). Answers are given in the appendix.

1. Behavioral, physical, and thinking components to anxiety influence each other in positive feedback loops.　　T　　F

2. Worrying is associated mostly with low levels of parasympathetic activity; fear is associated with peaks in sympathetic activity.　　T　　F

3. Worrying is an abnormal phenomenon that should be eliminated altogether.　　T　　F

4. Anxiety and worry always interfere with performance.　　T　　F

5. Worry and anxiety place the mind and body in a state of preparation for upcoming potential threats or challenges.　　T　　F

Chapter 4

A Closer Look at Generalized Anxiety Disorder

Goals

- To review your records from the previous week and add data to your Progress Record

- To learn what causes abnormal worry

- To continue record-keeping

- To complete the self-assessment

Review of Your Records

Did you complete your Worry Records and Daily Mood Records over the past week? Remember that it is vital for your success in this program that you continue to monitor your anxiety in the ways described. Once again, this helps you to develop an objective understanding of your own reactions and a full understanding of the triggers of your anxiety; the symptoms, thoughts, and behaviors most typical of your anxiety; and the positive feedback loops that escalate your anxiety. As we pointed out in chapter 2, it helps to stand outside of the bowl of gelatin rather than wallow in the middle of it. If you have not completed your records, we recommend that you spend at least a couple of days completing them and rereading the material in the last chapter before continuing.

If you did complete your records, add the number of anxiety episodes and the average maximum anxiety ratings to your Progress Record. Look to see if any patterns are developing. What are the typical events that trigger anxiety? What are your most typical thoughts and behaviors when you experience anxiety? Do you notice common themes in your worrisome thoughts, such as perfectionism or not wanting to make mistakes, or perhaps feeling responsible for everything that happens, either to yourself or to your loved ones? Which of the underlying beliefs listed in chapter 3 (perfectionism, responsibility, controllability, and negative beliefs about worry) is most relevant to your worry? Did you examine the sequences, or the cycling effects, among the components of anxiety? Did you notice ways in which your thoughts led to anxious behaviors or increased physical tension, which in turn, contributed to worrisome thoughts? Maybe you wake up feeling physically tense, and that leads you to be on the lookout for possible disasters during the day. Are you sometimes more aware of physical feelings, without being aware of obvious worries, or vice versa? Continuing to ask yourself these types of questions will help you gain a full and objective understanding of the nature of your anxiety reactions.

How Does Normal Worry Become Abnormal Worry?

There are really two questions to be addressed in this section. First, how does excessive worry and anxiety develop in the first place, or "Why did I become a worrier?" Second, what maintains excessive worry, or "Why can't I control this problem?"

Causes of Abnormal Worry

Understanding the initial causes of extreme anxiety and worry is not necessary in order to benefit from treatment, but it is helpful. A full understanding of the causes is not necessary because the factors that cause a problem to develop are not necessarily the same as the factors that keep the problem going.

Discovering the causes of anxiety is very difficult and is the focus of a great deal of scientific work. We do not know all of the answers yet. However, the research does not suggest that generalized anxiety is a disease or a specific biological or chemical dysfunction. On the other hand, as described in chapter 3, biological, physiological, and chemical processes are very much a part of the state of anxiety when it is present. So, what causes generalized anxiety?

There is good evidence that biological factors contribute to anxiety. Research has demonstrated an inherited component to feeling anxious, excitable, or tense, but this does not mean that GAD is genetic. What is probably inherited is a general sensitivity, or emotionality, that can be categorized as being "uptight," "high-strung," or "excitable." This type of sensitivity is not always unpleasant. For example, some people tend to get emotional at weddings or sporting events, and they actually enjoy these events more when they do "get into it." Therefore, having sensitivity or being emotional and reactive to positive and negative events is not necessarily a guarantee of an anxiety problem. It does seem, however, that being "high-strung" may be one of the factors that contributes to anxiety disorders.

What type of learning experiences contribute to becoming anxious? First is learning to view the world as a more dangerous and threatening place than other people do. Associated with this view of the world may be a set of beliefs concerning perfectionism, responsibility, and control (the underlying beliefs that make it difficult to stop worrying). That is, since threat is perceived to be ever-present, it makes sense that you would try to make everything "work" perfectly. It also makes sense that you would feel responsible for doing everything possible to prevent negative events (since, if you foresaw an event, but did nothing to prevent it, you would be to "blame") and to remain in control and on guard by worrying so that you can be ready to deal with dangers when they do arise, or even to prevent dangers. And how do we learn this? It seems that all of us, very early in life, develop a sense of whether we can cope with the unexpected, and sometimes challenging or stressful, events that we face. Healthy development during early childhood generates a sense that we can handle or control challenges and negative events, if they come along. If we do not develop this sense of control, perhaps due to an unfortunate series of unpleasant events in childhood or because as children we are constantly warned of the dangers that lurk around every corner, then we may develop a view of the world as a dangerous place and find ourselves always dwelling on the worst possible outcomes.

Remember, this type of view of the world does not, in and of itself, cause GAD; it just contributes to the chances of developing anxiety. Instead, a combination of biological and psychological factors is believed to explain anxiety problems.

Another feature of learning experiences that contribute to anxiety problems is stressors, or specific events that occur at specific points in time and trigger the development of an anxiety problem. On many occasions, patients seeking treatment report that they have always been somewhat more cautious than most people. In fact, being extra-prepared often led them to be more effective or productive in their functioning. However, when they left school, got married, had children, received a job promotion, lost a parent, or went through some other major positive or negative life experience, their anxiety intensified and became problematic. The anxiety increased and shifted from being a productive driving force to being a problematic, interfering force.

So, you can see how a complex interaction of several different factors can account for the development of excessive anxiety. The following diagram shows these factors. For a complete account of the recent research on the nature and causes of anxiety, you may wish to read *Anxiety and Its Disorders: The Nature and Treatment of Anxiety and Panic,* by David H. Barlow (New York: Guilford Press, 2002).

It is important to understand that having a higher level of emotionality or nervousness than others and being more likely to react strongly to life events is not a disease. Whether an anxiety problem develops is based on a complex interaction of the features that we already discussed: genetics and physiology, view of the world, and specific events that may occur. Also, it is important to understand that being an anxious person does not mean that you have some type of mental illness, but rather, it is a characteristic of your response that has developed over time. The sense of the world as being a dangerous and threatening place, the sense of responsibility, and

Interaction of Factors Causing Anxiety

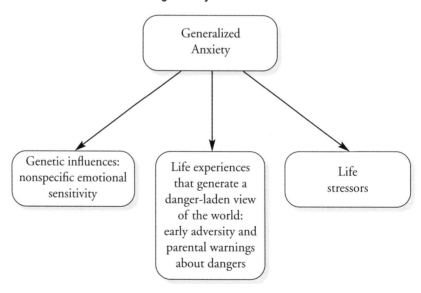

the striving for perfectionism and control are all aspects of your response that can be changed.

Remember that anxiety and worry are normal states that actually serve a protective function, by preparing us for upcoming uncertainties or threatening events. During this preparation, we experience physical tension and a stream of thoughts aimed at problem-solving. This process is important to our very survival. What makes worry abnormal is when it occurs at the wrong time—when no real threat or danger exists, when it is excessive, and when it never stops.

Factors That Maintain Anxiety

Once a state of heightened anxiety occurs, high levels of tension, anxious thoughts and images, and anxious behaviors maintain the problem. Remember, being in a state of high anxiety means that your body is in a state of physical preparation (a high level of tension) and your mind is in a state of readiness for danger and is attempting to engage in problem-solving ("what if"), even though these attempts are unsuccessful, and your behaviors are aimed at preventing bad things from happening or minimizing worry. The combination of worry, increased physical tension, and cautious behavior can keep anxiety going in the long term in several ways. As we described in chapter 3, anxious thoughts and behaviors and physical tension influence each other in positive feedback loops so as to generate more and more anxiety. These feedback loops also have consequences for anxiety in the long term and therefore contribute to the maintenance of anxiety. For example, worrying about meeting deadlines and having everything "just right" may motivate you to get everything done, but thoughts of "something going wrong" remain in the back of your mind. These thoughts can become so strong and overriding that they interfere with your ability to concentrate on what you're doing. Then, the next time you're faced with a deadline, you may have less confidence in your ability to concentrate and finish the task, thereby influencing your anxiety over the long term.

Also, high levels of tension may interfere with effective problem-solving, and instead, encourage you to focus on worst-case scenarios. Instead of problem-solving, you may focus on negative events as if they are likely, when in fact, the probability that they will occur is very low. In addition, you may blow things out of proportion by thinking that something will turn out to be a disaster, when in fact, it can be managed. Consequently, you may not give enough time or consideration to more realistic solutions.

Another reason that anxiety persists in the long term is related to the underlying beliefs that were discussed in chapter 3. These beliefs motivate continued worry or behaviors that eventually lead to continued worry. These beliefs include perfectionism, or the notion that one should not make mistakes and that to make mistakes is a sign of incompetence; responsibility, or the notion that it is irresponsible to dismiss worries about the possibility of negative events; control, or the notion that negative events can be prevented by worrying about them; and beliefs that excessive worry will cause you to go crazy, which leads to behaviors designed to decrease worry (such as distraction) that, in turn, contribute to the continuation of worry. Such attempts only make the worry stronger: The more you try not to think about a white elephant, the more likely it is that you will think about it. Resistance can be a very powerful reinforcer. Instead of resisting worries, it is more effective to challenge them and replace them with appropriate alternatives or solutions. Rather than trying to eliminate worry through distraction or by doing things that are designed to minimize worry (such as staying late at work to prepare for the next day), it is better to address worries directly by questioning the evidence and generating coping alternatives for the worst-case scenario. These types of challenges are described in detail in chapter 6.

Tension and worries can also persist when negative events that happen to all of us are interpreted as further justification for worry. That is, actual negative events may strengthen worry in someone who is already a worrier, due to the belief that if negative events happen once, they are more likely to happen in the future, and the belief that worry can somehow lessen the chance of future negative events (remember the issues of responsibility and control that were discussed earlier). An example might be, "Since I was reprimanded by my boss, I worry about being reprimanded again, and by worrying about being reprimanded, it is less likely to happen." Although worrying can sometimes lead to problem-solving behaviors that do reduce the chances of negative events (for example, worry about taking an exam leads to extra study that results in better performance), the belief that worry can prevent independent negative events is wrong. Try it. See if you can cause the number of traffic accidents in your area to decrease as a result of your worrying about them. In other words, the act of worrying has little effect on whether an independent negative event occurs. Similarly, worrying that the plane in which you are traveling may crash will not affect the probability of the plane crashing and worrying about the safety of your child who is living in another state or country will not affect the probability of injury or harm to your child.

A final reason someone with GAD continues to worry all the time when it doesn't solve any problems, and only makes things worse, relates to recent scientific discoveries. It seems that, if we engage in frantic, intense worry, our minds are so totally focused on thoughts of danger that it's not possible to focus on the feelings and images that underlie the rush of thoughts. In other words, we are thinking so hard about upcoming problems that we don't have time to really dwell on negative emotions in a productive way. This is because thinking about something and really feeling an emotion occupy different parts of our brains. But, letting ourselves experience emotions and feelings to the fullest is the only way for our emotions to eventually diminish. Thus, frantic worrying is a way to avoid dealing with the roots of the problem. The fact that this frantic worry process keeps us from dealing with the real problem is one of the reasons we keep doing it (even though we don't want to). Even though we know that the solution is to confront our real feelings and work through them, we constantly worry to avoid doing just that. One of the things you will learn to do in this program is to fully experience the images and emotions underlying your anxiety so that you can deal with them more effectively.

All of these factors contribute to the persistence of worry and tension. However, they can all be changed.

Factors That Maintain Excessive Anxiety and Worry

So far we have described (1) the intense spiral of anxiety episodes, due to interactions among the physical, behavioral, and cognitive components or response; (2) the initial causes of anxiety problems; and (3) the factors that maintain excessive anxiety and worry.

The Effects of Too Much Anxiety and Worry

While some anxiety can be a good thing, and even excessive anxiety, in the short term, can't hurt you, having generally high anxiety levels for long periods (or for many years) can take its toll. Anxiety will never make you go crazy, no matter how extreme, but being uptight for a long time can cause you to lose sleep, feel tired, have difficulty concentrating, and feel irritable. While these symptoms are not dangerous, they do make life less pleasant for you and those around you. They also lower your performance and productivity. This is why it is important to learn to control your excessive anxiety.

Long periods of excessive anxiety may affect your body. Having high levels of anxiety for long periods can increase the chance of heart disease, high blood pressure, diabetes, immune problems, and cancer later on in life. Stress and anxiety lower the functioning of your immune system and make you more susceptible to infectious diseases. Stress and anxiety can also interfere with your sexual functioning, so you may lose both your desire and your ability to function. There are also a number of physical problems that are mainly caused by high levels of chronic anxiety: irritable bowel syndrome, nervous stomach, frequent gas, diarrhea, ulcers, headaches, skin irritations, and temporomandibular joint dysfunction.

There is no need to be alarmed about these problems or to add more anxiety to your current level. Being highly anxious does not guarantee that you will have these diseases or problems, but anxiety can increase your chances of having them in the future. All of these facts mean that it is very worthwhile for you to learn to be less anxious.

Training Program Rationale: How to Learn to Be Less Anxious

This program will teach you how to change your current style of responding so that your anxiety is not excessive or chronic, although it will still be present in situations in which anxiety is useful. In essence, the program entails learning new ways of thinking, behaving, and reacting physically. The program targets each of the three components of anxiety: behavior, physical reactions, and thoughts. You will learn how to change the kind of statements and negative predictions that you make, and particularly, how to control your worry. In addition, you will be taught how to decrease your physical symptoms. Then, you will learn how to face the fearful emotions that underlie your worry and how to engage in certain tasks that you currently avoid for fear of negative outcomes. These tasks are designed to prove your negative predictions false and to help you change your behaviors.

We will begin with the methods of physical control, since methods of physical relaxation will become a natural part of your daily routine. It is essential to take some time each day for relaxation. You will be learning a method of relaxation that has proven to be very valuable for many people; it is called "progressive muscle relaxation." Learning relaxation techniques will decrease the level of physical tension that is contributing to the maintenance of your anxiety problems, as well as provide a tool for interrupting the escalating cycle during an anxiety episode.

Then, we will focus on the kinds of self-statements you make and the negative predictions that guide your feelings and behaviors. You will be taught methods of counteracting your negative predictions, as well as how to develop more realistic predictions that will become as powerful and automatic as your negative predictions are right now. Next, we will focus on identifying underlying emotions and associated catastrophic images, and then, through a series of structured exercises, we will help you to face those emotions and images so that they subside.

Next, you will do direct behavioral practice of two types. First, you will be taught to change your safety-checking behavior so that you learn that the dangers you predict are not going to happen, even if you do not check. Second, you will be taught to engage in activities that you may have been avoiding because of your negative predictions or your frantic, chronic worry, to learn that either nothing bad happens or that the worst that happens can be managed.

Finally, you will be taught methods of effective problem-solving to deal with real negative events. As a result of these procedures, you will be able to dismiss your negative thoughts because you know that they are unfounded.

Homework

✎ Consolidate all of the information given so far before going ahead with the actual skills learning.

✎ Reread this and the previous chapter several times.

✎ Continue with your record-keeping, using the Worry Record and the Daily Mood Record.

✎ Once you feel that you really understand the material and the program for treatment, begin the next chapter.

Self-Assessment

Answer each of the following questions by circling T (true) or F (false). Answers are given in the appendix.

1. People are born with generalized anxiety disorder and all that treatment does is help them to accept their state. T F

2. Emotional sensitivity means that some people are more reactive to events, but does not mean that an anxiety disorder will necessarily develop. T F

3. There is no evidence that a specific biological dysfunction causes generalized anxiety disorder, although biological and physiological processes are part of the experience of anxiety. T F

4. Learning to worry less means becoming less responsible. T F

5. Being an anxious person means that I will always experience high, excessive anxiety. T F

6. Although high levels of anxiety over long periods can increase the chance of certain physical problems in the future, an episode of anxiety is unlikely to cause any immediate harm. T F

Chapter 5   *Learning to Relax*

Goals

- To review your records from the previous week and add data to your Progress Record

- To learn progressive muscle relaxation training

- To fill out the Relaxation Record on a weekly basis

- To continue record-keeping

- To complete the self-assessment

Review of Your Records

Before you start this chapter, review your Worry Records and Daily Mood Record. If you have stopped keeping your records, remember that recording your thoughts, behaviors, and symptoms is an essential part of this program. Without the records, you will not be able to evaluate your own reactions or tailor the anxiety control strategies to your own particular anxiety. So, it is really to your benefit to continue the record-keeping. In addition, we recommend that you do not continue until you fully understand all of the material presented in the previous chapters. If you have questions, either reread the section or ask your mental health professional for clarification. Since so much of this program is based on learning new principles, it is very important that you fully understand the reasons for everything that you will be asked to do.

From your records, what do you notice about the previous week? In particular, what are the typical themes of your worry, and what are the positive feedback loops among your thoughts, physical symptoms, and behaviors? Add the number of episodes of anxiety and average maximum anxiety ratings to the Progress Record. Do not worry if the averages have not changed yet. You are still in the learning phase of this program. The application phase will begin with this chapter.

Progressive Muscle Relaxation

In the previous chapter, physical tension was described as one of the factors that both contributes to and results from worry and anxiety. For this reason, learning to relax physically is one pathway to interrupting the cycle of anxiety and worry.

People relax in many different ways. Some people sit quietly and listen to music, and others practice yoga or some other form of meditation. A procedure that we find to be very useful is called "progressive muscle relaxation training."

This method has two components: one for physical relaxation and one for mental relaxation. Physical relaxation is taught through a series of muscular tensing and releasing exercises. It begins with 16 different muscle groups, and then, with practice, decreases to eight muscle groups, and then to four muscle groups, before finally being reduced to relaxation in one step. Mental relaxation is taught through learning to focus your attention on the sensations that you experience during the tensing and releasing exercises.

Initially, the procedure takes approximately 30 minutes. As the number of specific muscle groups is reduced, the procedure becomes shorter. Eventually, the goal is to relax in one step. However, as with any new behavioral procedure, relaxation is a skill that takes considerable practice. Therefore, achieving one-step relaxation requires time and effort.

The advantage of the one-step method of relaxation is that it can be used to interrupt anxiety as soon as tension starts to build. However, the lengthier, more extensive 30-minute version of relaxation is a very useful general strategy for letting go of tension that has accumulated during the day. Even though you will learn how to shorten the relaxation procedure progressively so that it can become an applied skill, it will be valuable to continue to practice the longer versions as well.

As described in the last chapter, the combination of high levels of physical tension and negative thinking contribute to the persistence of worry and anxiety. By learning a method to reduce your level of physical tension, it will be easier for you to control your worrying. Relaxation should become a regular part of your daily schedule. Your initial response might be, "I don't have time to relax. There are far too many other things that have to get done!" This sense of time pressure only adds to your anxiety. Changing your schedule and taking the time to relax will not only lower physical tension, but also will teach you a very important lesson, which is that most of the things you believe have to get done can wait.

Now let's discuss the procedure itself. By the way, if you are already using a specific relaxation strategy that you find effective, it's not necessary for you to learn the procedure we describe here. Nevertheless, you should read through the remainder of the relaxation sections of this book to ensure that you are following all of the principles. Also, if you have tried one form of relaxation and it did not work, don't assume that it will not work this time. It may not have worked for a lot of reasons that you were not fully aware of, but that can be corrected with practice.

Initially, the exercise involves tensing the muscles, followed by releasing or relaxing. The tensing has two purposes. First, the tension-relaxation procedure acts like a pendulum: the further you pull it one way (tension), the further it will go the other way (relaxation), and therefore, relaxation is made easier. Second, the tensing exercises provide a strong contrast with the relaxation part of the procedure so that you can learn to discriminate very clearly between tension and relaxation. Sometimes tension builds gradually, without our awareness. Learning to detect the initial signs of an increase in tension will put you in a better position to use relaxation as a tool early on, rather than waiting for anxiety and tension to reach high levels.

The tensing part of the exercises is not intended to produce pain. In fact, if you experience chronic pain in any part of your body, it is best to avoid the tensing component for the muscles in that area; just do the relaxing component when you get to those muscle groups.

The procedure asks you to tense and release different muscle groups in sequence. We start with the arms and then move to the legs, stomach, chest, shoulders, neck, and face. During the tensing part of the exercises, you should tense only the specified muscle group, keeping the rest of your body relaxed. Of course, some overlap is unavoidable; for example, it is difficult to avoid tensing your lower arms when you tense your upper arms. However, some parts of your body can fairly easily remain relaxed as you tense other parts of your body; for example, it is easy to relax your face and your legs as you tense your arms.

Throughout the exercise, concentrate on the sensations produced by tensing and releasing different muscle groups. You can do this by repeatedly telling yourself, "Think about the feelings in my arm, feel the tension and tightness. . . . Feel the warmth of releasing the tension." Other thoughts may enter your mind, particularly worrisome thoughts. Don't get upset or try to get rid of these thoughts. Instead, gently bring your concentration back to the physical sensations. By redirecting your attention, you will learn to dismiss worrisome thoughts; that is, even though the worrisome thoughts may still be present, the fact that you are not giving them all of your attention and, instead, directing your attention to the physical sensations of relaxation, will mean that you are teaching yourself that those worrisome thoughts are not important and that you are not controlled by them.

As with the learning of any new skill, it is helpful to begin practicing in environments in which you will not be distracted and at times that you have specifically set aside for relaxation. Later on, you will be asked to practice relaxing in more distracting places, so that you can eventually use relaxation as a strategy wherever you are when you notice tension building. For the moment, however, find a quiet place where you know you will not be distracted or disturbed. If you have children, do the relaxation exercise when they are asleep, at school, or being looked after by someone else. A high-backed, comfortable chair that provides support for your neck is ideal, but lying on a bed is okay, as long as you do not fall asleep. Loosen tight clothing, including shoes or belts, and uncross your legs or arms. If you wear glasses or contact lenses, remove them before going ahead with the exercise.

The following exercise should be practiced every day, twice a day, for the next seven days. Initially, that means 30 minutes twice a day. This is necessary in order to really learn how to relax. Do not expect major changes at first. With practice, you will feel the effects of relaxation.

Read the following set of instructions very carefully. If possible, record the instructions on an audiotape. When you're ready to practice, you can follow your own taped instructions.

The Relaxation Procedure

Get into a comfortable position, close your eyes, and sit quietly for a few seconds, taking some slow, deep breaths.

1. Build up the tension in your lower arms by making fists with your hands and pulling up on your wrists. If your nails are long, press your fingers against your palms to make fists. Feel the tension through your lower arms, wrists, fingers, knuckles, and hands. Focus on the tension. Notice the sensations of pulling, of discomfort, of tightness. Hold the tension (10 seconds). Now, release the tension and let your hands and lower arms relax onto the chair or bed, with your palms facing down. Focus your attention on the sensations of relaxation in your hands and arms. Feel the release from tension. Relax the muscles (20 seconds), and as you relax, breathe smoothly and slowly from your abdomen. Each time you exhale, think the word "relax."

2. Now, build up the tension in your upper arms by pulling your arms back and in, toward your sides. Feel the tension in the back of your arms and radiating up into your shoulders and back. Focus on the sensations of tension. Hold the tension (10 seconds). Now, release your arms and let them relax. Focus on your upper arms, and feel the difference compared with the tension. Your arms might feel heavy, warm, and relaxed. As you relax (20 seconds), breathe smoothly and slowly from your abdomen. Each time you exhale, think the word "relax."

3. Now, build up the tension in your lower legs by flexing your feet and pulling your toes toward your upper body. Feel the tension as it spreads through your feet, ankles, shins, and calves. Focus on the tension spreading down the back of your leg, into your foot, under your foot, and around your toes. Concentrate on that part of your body (10 seconds). Now, release the tension. Let your legs relax heavily onto the chair or bed. Feel the difference in the muscles as they relax. Feel the release from tension, the sense of comfort, and the warmth and heaviness of relaxation (20 seconds). As you breathe smoothly and slowly, think the word "relax" each time you exhale.

4. Build up the tension in your upper legs by pulling your knees together and lifting your legs off of the bed or chair. Focus on the

tightness in your upper legs. Feel the pulling sensations from the hip down, and notice the tension in your legs. Focus on that part of your body (10 seconds). Now, release the tension, and let your legs drop down heavily onto the chair or bed. Let the tension go away. Concentrate on the feeling of relaxation. Feel the difference in your legs. Focus on the feeling of comfort (20 seconds), and as you breathe smoothly and slowly, think the word "relax" each time you exhale.

5. Now, build up the tension in your stomach by pulling your stomach in toward your spine very tightly. Feel the tension. Feel the tightness, and focus on that part of your body (10 seconds). Now, let your stomach relax outwards. Let it go further and further. Feel the sense of warmth circulating across your stomach. Feel the comfort of relaxation (20 seconds). As you breathe smoothly and slowly, think the word "relax" each time you exhale.

6. Now, build up the tension around your chest by taking a deep breath and holding it. Your chest is expanded, and the muscles are stretched around it. Feel the tension in your chest and back. Hold your breath (10 seconds). Now, slowly, let the air escape and breathe normally, letting the air flow in and out smoothly and easily. Feel the difference as the muscles relax compared with the tension, and think the word "relax" each time you exhale.

7. Imagine that your shoulders are on strings and are pulled up toward your ears. Feel the tension around your shoulders, radiating down into your back and up into your neck and the back of your head. Focus on this part of your body. Concentrate on the sensations around your neck and shoulders (10 seconds), and then let your shoulders droop. Relax and let them droop further and further. Feel the sense of relaxation around your neck and shoulders. Concentrate on the sensation of relaxation (20 seconds) in this part of your body. As you breathe smoothly and slowly, think the word "relax" each time you exhale.

8. Build up the tension around your neck by pressing the back of your neck toward the chair or bed and pulling your chin down toward your chest. Feel the tightness around the back of your neck spreading up into the back of your head. Focus on the tension (10 seconds). Now, release the tension, letting your head rest comfortably against the bed or chair. Concentrate on the relaxation (20 seconds), and feel

the difference from the tension. As you breathe smoothly and slowly, think the word "relax" each time you exhale.

9. Build up the tension around your mouth, jaw, and throat by clenching your teeth and forcing the corners of your mouth back into a forced smile (10 seconds). Feel the tightness, and concentrate on the sensations. Then, release the tension, letting your mouth drop open and the muscles around your throat and jaw relax. Concentrate on the difference in the sensations in that part of your body (20 seconds). As you breathe smoothly and slowly, think the word "relax" each time you exhale.

10. Build up the tension around your eyes by squeezing your eyes tightly shut for a few seconds, and then releasing. Then, let the tension around your eyes slide away. Feel the difference as the muscles relax (20 seconds). As you breathe smoothly and slowly, think the word "relax" each time you exhale.

11. Build up the tension across your lower forehead by frowning, pulling your eyebrows down and toward the center. Feel the tension across your forehead and the top of your head. Concentrate on the tension (10 seconds), and then release, smoothing out the wrinkles and letting your forehead relax. Feel the difference as you relax (20 seconds). As you breathe smoothly and slowly, think the word "relax" each time you exhale.

12. Build up the tension across your upper forehead by raising your eyebrows as high as you can. Feel the wrinkling and pulling sensations across your forehead and the top of your head. Hold the tension (10 seconds), and then relax, letting your eyebrows rest and the tension leave. Concentrate on the sensations of relaxation, and feel the difference in comparison to tension. As you breathe smoothly and slowly, think the word "relax" each time you exhale.

13. Now your whole body is feeling relaxed and comfortable. As you feel yourself becoming even more relaxed, count from one to five. One, letting all of the tension leave your body. Two, sinking further and further into relaxation. Three, feeling more and more relaxed. Four, feeling very relaxed. Five, feeling deeply relaxed. As you spend a few minutes in this relaxed state, think about your breathing. Feel the cool air as you breathe in and the warm air as you breathe out. Your breathing is slow and regular. Every time you breathe out, think the

word "relax" (2 minutes). Now, count backward from five, gradually feeling yourself become more alert and awake. Five, feeling more awake. Four, coming out of the relaxation. Three, feeling more alert. Two, opening your eyes. One, sitting up.

Once you learn to do this set of exercises, it is very possible that you will lower your heart rate and blood pressure. For that reason, do not stand up quickly afterward. Now, practice the exercise.

After going through the full set of tensing and releasing exercises, evaluate your experience. Were there any parts of your body that were difficult to relax? For very tense parts of your body, it may help to tense and release several times. Were you able to focus your attention? Remember that equally important as physical relaxation is mental relaxation, or learning to shift your attention away from worrisome thoughts and onto the physical sensations associated with the tension and relaxation exercises. If other thoughts enter your mind, let them pass, and redirect your attention to the physical sensations of relaxation. It doesn't matter if the worrisome thoughts remain in the back of your mind—you are teaching yourself that those worrisome thoughts do not deserve your full attention.

Did you feel anxiety during the procedure? You may experience an initial increase in anxiety as you follow the relaxation exercises, for a number of reasons. Unusual sensations, such as a floating sensation or a sinking feeling, sometimes occur as a result of deep relaxation, and these sensations may produce anxiety, although they are normal and harmless. Sometimes the sense of "letting go" is disturbing initially. Again, this may take some getting used to, especially if you usually tend to be on edge, vigilant, and ready for any possibility. "Letting go" will feel unfamiliar at first, and perhaps a little threatening. However, with practice, you will learn that negative events are not more likely to occur, just because you allow yourself to relax. Another reason that relaxation will sometimes increase anxiety is that you may be worrying about things that you should be doing while you're attempting to relax. In this case, practice dismissing these thoughts and shifting your attention back to the sensations of tensing and relaxing your muscles. If you did become anxious as a result of the relaxation technique, you should continue practicing the exercise regardless. With repetition, your anxiety will decrease and you will feel the true effects of relaxation.

Keep a record of your relaxation practice on the Relaxation Record so that you can evaluate your progress. Use a new Relaxation Record for each week over the next several weeks. On the record, note the level of relaxation that you achieve by the end of the exercise (on a 0- to 100-point scale, where 0 = no relaxation and 100 = excellent relaxation). Also, rate your average degree of concentration during the procedure (using a 0- to 100-point scale, where 0 = no concentration and 100 = excellent concentration). Remember, concentration refers to focusing on the sensations of tension and relaxation. The Relaxation Record lists two practices for each day. Obviously, the goal is for the ratings of relaxation and concentration to increase with practice. If they do not increase, consider the possibilities listed earlier; perhaps you're trying too hard to relax, maybe you're becoming frustrated because you are thinking about too many other things that "should" get done, or perhaps you are uncomfortable with the idea of "letting go."

After you have practiced the relaxation procedure for seven days and are able to achieve at least moderate relaxation (at least 50 on the 0- to 100-point scale), move to the eight-muscle-group procedure (described later) for one of your two daily practices. That is, for one of your daily practices, continue to use the 16-muscle-group procedure, and use the eight-muscle-group procedure for the other one. On the other hand, if you are experiencing difficulty relaxing, or if you have not practiced enough, continue to use the 16-muscle-group procedure for both daily practices for another seven days.

The end goal is to achieve one-step relaxation. The first move toward that goal is the eight-muscle-group exercise, which is the same as the 16-muscle-group procedure, except that certain muscles are excluded. We suggest the following muscle groups for the eight-muscle-group procedure: (1) arms, combining lower and upper arms; (2) legs, combining lower and upper leg's; (3) stomach; (4) chest; (5) shoulders; (6) neck; (7) eyes; and (8) forehead (either upper or lower). However, if another area of your body typically becomes very tense, then replace one of the recommended muscle groups with that one. Use the same tensing and relaxing procedures, focusing your attention on the sensations, and progressing from one muscle group to another. During each relaxation phase, repeat the word "relax" as you exhale. Eventually, that word will become a strong cue, or trigger, for relaxation. Count from 1 to 5 to become more relaxed, relax, and breathe slowly for a couple of minutes. Then count backward from 5 to 1 as you gradually return to an alert state. As before, practice the eight-muscle-group relaxation procedure, daily, and keep a record of your practices on the Relaxation Record. Monitoring will provide feedback for yourself and anyone you're working with. An outline of the relaxation procedures is shown.

Relaxation Record

Rate relaxation and concentration at the end of each practice, using the following scale:

0 ----- 10 ----- 20 ----- 30 ----- 40 ----- 50 ----- 60 ----- 70 ----- 80 ----- 90 ----- 100

None   Mild   Moderate   Strong   Excellent

Date	Practice	Relaxation at the End of the Exercise	Concentration During the Exercise
	1		
	2		
	1		
	2		
	1		
	2		
	1		
	2		
	1		
	2		
	1		
	2		
	1		
	2		

Outline for Progressive Muscle Relaxation

1. Choose a quiet location, with a comfortable chair or bed.

2. Loosen tight clothing, and remove glasses or contact lenses.

3. Tense for 10 seconds and relax for 20 seconds, repeating the word "relax" silently to yourself on each exhalation, for the following major muscle groups:

    1, 2   Lower arms

    3, 4   Upper arms

    5, 6   Lower legs

    7, 8   Upper legs

    9   Abdomen

    10   Chest

    11   Shoulders

    12   Neck

    13   Mouth, throat, and jaw

    14   Eyes

    15   Lower forehead

    16   Upper forehead

4. Focus your attention on the sensations of tension and relaxation.

5. After tensing and releasing the 16 muscle groups, count from 1 to 5 to deepen relaxation, and breathe slowly for 2 minutes, repeating the word "relax" with every exhalation. Then count from 5 to 1 to return to a state of alertness.

6. Practice twice a day, for seven days.

7. Monitor your practice using the Relaxation Record.

8. Proceed to the eight-muscle-group procedure when you can achieve at least moderate relaxation with the 16-muscle-group procedure. Use the same exercises with the following muscle groups:

    1   Upper and lower arms

    2   Upper and lower legs

3 Abdomen

4 Chest

5 Shoulders

6 Neck

7 Eyes

8 Forehead

9. Practice the eight- and 16-muscle-group procedures once daily each, for seven days.

Special Issues

The relaxation exercise may be difficult at first. We have already mentioned some of the difficulties that can arise with relaxation, and we summarize them and other common difficulties in this section:

1. *Frustration and rushing.* Sometimes, frustration develops as a result of not feeling the immediate effects of relaxation or from trying to "squeeze" in a relaxation practice in between many other tasks. To manage this frustration, remember that it would be rare for anyone to feel the effects of relaxation immediately; practice effects build slowly. Also, trying to fit relaxation in between other tasks that you believe must get done only intensifies the tension, and will almost guarantee that the procedure will not be relaxing. Set aside a specific time to relax, and be sure to give yourself plenty of time. Remember, some of the things that you feel should get done immediately probably can wait.

2. *Concentration.* Sometimes keeping one's mind on the task, particularly for the full 30 minutes, is difficult. However, it is important to let go of other thoughts, images, or worries that enter your mind. Simply tell yourself to concentrate on what you're feeling, as if you were giving a running commentary on your physical experiences.

3. *Increased anxiety.* As mentioned earlier, you may experience anxiety while attempting to relax. Sometimes this is due to feeling out of control, or letting down one's guard, and sometimes it is related to feeling new, and perhaps troublesome, sensations (such as a sensation

of floating). Remember that these sensations, which may seem odd to you, are completely normal. Also, remember that it is okay to let down your guard. You are not at risk for more negative events just by being more relaxed.

4. *Falling asleep.* Sometimes people fall asleep when they practice relaxing. This does not help you to learn an applied skill, and so it should be avoided as much as possible. Practice the relaxation exercises at times when you are not tired.

Homework

✎ Continue to monitor your levels of anxiety, using the Worry Event Record and the Daily Mood Record.

✎ Continue to observe your episodes of anxiety in terms of the behavioral, physical, and thinking response components, and the ways in which they interact.

✎ Practice the 16-muscle-group relaxation procedure twice daily for the next seven days, recording your practices using the Relaxation Record.

✎ After seven days, evaluate your progress. If your relaxation ratings are mostly less than 50, then continue the same 16-muscle-group procedure for another seven days. If your relaxation ratings are mostly 50 or higher, then start practicing the eight-muscle-group procedure for one of your daily practices, for seven days, using the 16-muscle-group procedure for the other daily practice

Self-Assessment

Answer each of the following questions by circling T (true) or F (false). Answers are given in the appendix.

1. The goal of relaxation training is to reduce the levels of physical tension.   T   F

2. Practice should be done whenever time is available.   T   F

3. Relaxation procedures have two components: physical relaxation and mental relaxation.   T   F

4. As much as possible, one should concentrate on the feelings of tension and relaxation as one progresses from one muscle group to the next.   T   F

5. If I do not feel relaxed immediately, then I must be doing something wrong.   T   F

Goals

- To review your records from the previous week and add data to your Progress Record

- To learn the four-muscle-group relaxation technique

- To learn to change anxious patterns of thinking

- To practice self-statement training

- To continue record-keeping

- To begin using the Worry Record—Real Odds form

- To complete the self-assessment

Review of Your Records

Check your Worry Records and Daily Mood Record ratings since the last time you added summary data to the Progress Record, which may have been one or two weeks ago. Add the number of anxiety episodes you've had per week and the average maximum anxiety rating to your Progress Record. Has the practice of relaxation influenced your daily levels of anxiety? Has the number of anxiety episodes changed, or have your maximum anxiety ratings decreased?

What about your practice of relaxation? Were you able to practice twice almost every day? If not, evaluate the reasons. Some of the more commonly reported reasons for not practicing include: (1) being too busy or unexpectedly being faced with many tasks that were not anticipated; (2) not believing that the relaxation exercise would actually reduce anxiety; and (3) feeling frustrated because the relaxation exercise did not produce an immediate sense of overall calmness. If you did not practice relaxation because you were too busy, remember that a sense of time pressure and trying to get everything done at once is likely to contribute to ongoing anxiety. The extent to which that pressure is necessary (does everything really have to get done immediately?) will be addressed in this and the next few chapters. At the very least, however, the feeling that you do not have enough time in the day to get everything done is probably a good sign that, for you, it is important to take time out to relax. If you did not practice relaxing because you were doubtful about whether it would decrease your anxiety, remember that any new technique should not be judged until it has been given a fair trial. We included this technique because many people have found it to be very helpful in reducing their anxiety. If you stopped practicing relaxation because the exercise did not lower your levels of anxiety immediately, remember that relaxation is a skill that requires practice. Do not expect it to be effective immediately. Continue to practice, and you will feel the effects gradually.

Relaxation Practice

If you have not already started the eight-muscle-group relaxation procedure, do so for the next week (see chapter 5 for instructions). If you have practiced the eight-muscle-group procedure with good results (that is, you are able to achieve at least a moderate level of relaxation and a moderate level of concentration during the exercises), then progress to the four-muscle-group procedure that is described next.

The four-muscle-group procedure uses the same principles as the sixteen- and 8-muscle-group procedures, except that fewer muscles are targeted. Research shows that the same general body relaxation effects occur with the four-muscle-group procedure, after enough practice with the 16- and 8-muscle-group procedures. The four muscle groups that we recommend include the abdomen, chest, shoulders, and forehead. Of course, you may add other muscle groups or replace these muscles with other muscle groups in which you experience a lot of tension. As before, tense and release each muscle group, pairing the relaxation phase with the word "relax" on each exhalation. Then deepen the relaxation state by counting from 1 to 5, focus on your breathing for several minutes, and then count backward from 5 to 1. Review the outline in chapter 5 to remind yourself of the steps of relaxation. As before, we recommend that you practice the shortened procedure (four-muscle-group procedure) once a day, while continuing to practice the 16-muscle-group procedure (for the full 30 minutes) once a day also. In this way, you will achieve two goals. First, you are moving closer and closer to a one-step method of relaxation that you can use as soon as you notice tension and anxiety building. Second, you will establish relaxation as a regular part of your daily schedule. Remember to record your degree of relaxation and concentration for every time you practice, using the Relaxation Record.

Introduction to Changing Anxious Thinking

Now that you have started to learn a method of controlling physical tension, it's time to learn how to change anxious patterns of thinking. Thoughts play a major role in how different emotional states are experienced. In this case, we are most concerned with the particular thoughts that contribute to anxiety and worry.

The following example shows how beliefs (or thoughts) can influence our behavior and emotional states. Picture yourself walking with friends through a dense forest. Let's say that your walk begins very pleasantly, as you enjoy the unusual wildlife and plants and the sounds of birds in the trees above. You feel relaxed and comfortable as you explore the scenery around you. Then, one of your friends tells you that that he thought he saw a poisonous snake. Now you believe that a dangerous snake is crawling in the grass. Rustling sounds that you had ignored before take on a very different meaning, and become the focus of your attention. You begin to move more cautiously, as images of the snake biting you without warning race through your mind. You think about ways of getting out of the forest and reaching safety. Your heart rate and breathing rate increase, because your body is in a state of preparation or readiness for when the snake appears.

This example shows how perceived danger (thoughts of the poisonous snake) can have a dramatic effect. Such thoughts naturally lead us to become very tense, on guard for anything that we believe might signal danger (such as rustling sounds). We also look for safety. These reactions would have occurred, regardless of whether a snake was actually in the grass, as long as one *believed* that the snake was nearby.

By extension, it is easy to see how worry and physical tension can result from viewing negative events as being likely to occur. For example, if you were concerned that your husband or wife might be injured or killed in a car accident on the way home from work, then you would feel tense, be on guard, listen to news reports about road conditions and car accidents, wait by the phone in case the police try to reach you, and stop your usual activities until you are assured of his or her safety.

The key question is whether your judgment of danger or threat is valid. The actual risk is an empirical issue, one that needs to be examined by looking at the facts. If you discover that your worries are not fully supported by facts, you can reevaluate and discount the worries. In this way, the associated anxiety will decrease. Questioning the evidence, in many cases, will result in the recognition that your worries are unfounded.

Why do you worry about events for which there is little or no evidence? One reason might be a tendency to view the world as dangerous, as we discussed in chapter 4. That is, it becomes a habit to think of the things that could go wrong. Another reason is that the more physically tense you feel, the more likely it is that you will have worrisome thoughts about negative events, which in turn generate more physical tension, and so on. These are the positive feedback loops we described in chapter 3. Another reason is the belief that, if a worrisome thought or negative image occurs, then it must be taken seriously rather than dismissed; this, too, is likely to contribute to worrying about events for which there is little direct evidence.

Remember, we have described worry as an attempt at problem-solving because of a sense of perceived risk or danger. However, instead of constructively solving the problem, a person who worries excessively sees only negative outcomes. Along with evaluating whether the negative event you are worried about is a real possibility, it is important to develop a set of alternatives or problem-solving solutions, in case the negative outcomes occur.

To illustrate these strategies, let's consider the earlier description of worrying that your husband or wife will be injured or die on the way home from work. First, examine the evidence concerning the possibility that your spouse will be involved in a car accident at that point in time. Assuming that your spouse has a good driving record, and considering the number of accidents relative to the number of people driving on any given day, the real probability of your spouse being involved in an accident may be very low, in which case your worry is out of proportion to the evidence. Second, to develop alternative solutions to the worst possible outcome, picture the worst happening and then consider ways of coping. Although this is easier to do with less significant events, such as making a mistake at work, than with more significant events, such as the loss of a spouse, the principles remain the same. Even under the worst circumstances, there is something that can be done.

General Principles for Changing Your Anxious Thinking (Self-Statement Training)

There are several basic principles for self-statement training.

1. First, challenging your negative thoughts does not mean just "positive thinking." You will not need to replace all of your negative thoughts with positive thoughts. Positive thinking is just as inaccurate as negative thinking. Instead, you will examine all of the evidence available to you, in an effort to balance your thinking and interpretations by using a realistic perspective. Sometimes negative events do happen, and therefore, positive thinking can be unadaptive and get in the way of problem-solving. However, negative events probably occur less often than you are predicting, and with fewer negative consequences than you are imagining.

2. Worrisome thoughts and images tend to become habitual and almost automatic. For example, a woman who was treated at our clinic reported that she always made sure that her house was clean and tidy by mid-morning, just in case friends or neighbors dropped by unexpectedly. It was not until she asked herself why it was important to have a "perfect" house that she realized that she automatically assumed that people would disapprove of her if her house wasn't in "perfect" order. Observing your own behaviors will help you to discover your underlying beliefs and assumptions.

3. Finally, although beliefs and self-statement patterns can become habitual, they are not impossible to change. With the right kind of effort and experience, we can change our views and beliefs about the world and ourselves just as we can change our religious beliefs or our language. Of course, this type of change takes practice and effort.

Beginning to Change Your Anxious Thinking (Self-Statement Analysis)

As a first step, it is essential to know exactly what it is that you tell yourself in different situations. The more specifically you can describe your thoughts, the easier it will be to correct or challenge your assumptions.

For example, simply stating, "I am worried about my child getting sick," is not specific enough. Instead, ask yourself about the details of the worrisome thought. What do you think might happen if your child were to become sick? Do you think your child might die or be disabled for life? Do you worry that his or her sickness means that you have failed as a parent? Do you worry that his or her sickness would be unbearable? The following is a description of how a therapist is helping a client, Joan, to describe her thoughts and worries more specifically:

Therapist: You said that you are constantly worried about others watching you at work. What is it that you're worried that they might see? And what leads you to assume that they're watching you?

Joan: I feel like they're watching to see that I'm doing everything that I'm supposed to be doing . . . that I'm not making mistakes.

Therapist: What kind of mistakes?

Joan: Well, for example, typing errors and wasting time retyping letters over and over again.

Therapist: Do you often retype letters over and over again?

Joan: No, actually, believe it or not, I'm a pretty good typist. I guess it's just that I worry that if I did make a mistake, they would see it.

Therapist: And what if they did notice that you made a mistake? Then what?

Joan: Well, I would worry that they might tell my boss.

Therapist: Go on. What next?

Joan: Well, my boss would either keep an eye on me continually or ask me to leave, and then I'd be without a job. I don't want to lose my job.

Therapist: So, the bottom line for why you're concerned that others are watching you is that you could be fired. Anyone who believed that they were about to lose their job would most likely feel some anxiety. We need to examine whether the evidence is consistent with you being fired, such as whether your colleagues really are watching you, what they would actually do if they did notice a mistake, and what your boss would actually do if someone mentioned that you had made a mistake.

As an exercise, choose three to four examples from your Worry Records over the past two weeks. Now, think back to those events, and read the anxious thoughts that you recorded. Can you expand on those thoughts and provide a more detailed description of what you thought might happen or what you were worried about? Ask yourself the kind of questions that the therapist asked Joan. What, specifically, did you think could have happened? In the following example, Joan describes her worries about her boyfriend, Rob.

> When Rob didn't call me last night, I thought it was because he didn't like me anymore, or that I wasn't good enough for him. I thought that it was the end of our relationship, and that I would never see him again. Then I'd have to explain to all my friends what happened. My friends would feel sorry for me, and that would make me feel even worse, because they would think of me as someone who is never going to be in a stable relationship. What is even worse is that I think they might be right. I'm never going to meet someone who really cares for me.

As you can see, Joan is not just worried that her boyfriend doesn't like her, but that she will never meet anyone and that her friends will judge her to be incapable of ever meeting anyone. Notice how Joan assumed the worst and did not consider possible alternatives for why her boyfriend didn't call her. Perhaps he was tired, or upset with her, or out with friends, none of which necessarily means the end of the relationship. Also notice how Joan then extended her worry from the end of this relationship to never having a relationship. That sounds like jumping to conclusions. Similarly, her worry that her friends would judge her poorly if her relationship with Bob ended sounds like another example of jumping to conclusions.

Judgments of Risk

Errors in judgment tend to occur whenever someone is in a state of high anxiety. First, we tend to overestimate the likelihood of negative events happening. Second, we tend to view the consequences of negative events as being catastrophic and unmanageable. In short, we think the worst. Of course, as you probably understand by now, this type of error in judgment only increases our anxiety. So, the very first step in correcting your thinking is to recognize that whenever you feel anxious, you are probably overestimating, catastrophizing, or both.

In this chapter, we focus on the first error in judgment, which is to overestimate the likelihood of negative events or jump to conclusions. In the next lesson, we focus on catastrophizing, or blowing things out of proportion. A good example of overestimation was reported in a study in England some years ago (Butler & Mathews, 1983). The researchers assessed a group of university students one month before and one day before a major exam. Each time, the students were asked to judge the likelihood that they would fail the exam. Interestingly, despite having a full month to study and prepare, many of the students rated the possibility of failure as much higher one day before the exam compared with one month earlier. The students overestimated the chance of failure because they were more anxious the day before the exam.

Overestimating the risk means jumping to conclusions about a particular event, and believing that it will happen, even though the actual odds are very low. From the earlier example, we could say that Joan was not likely to be fired although she felt as if it were a strong possibility. She was overlooking the fact that she was a good typist and other people were probably not evaluating her in the way that she assumed. Similarly, the likelihood that Joan would never meet anyone who really cared for her, or that her friends would judge her incapable of sustaining a relationship, was not supported by the evidence. Joan had just jumped to those conclusions.

Go back to the examples that you chose from your Worry Records over the last couple of weeks. Were any of those episodes of anxiety related to overestimating the likelihood of negative events? Were you judging something to be a high probability, only to find that it did not occur? This will be very apparent if you typically worry about the same thing over and over, yet it has never happened. Have you worried about your children being kidnapped, and how many times has that happened? Have you worried about missing appointments, and how many times has that happened? Have you worried about your neighbors being unfriendly to you because your house was untidy, and how many times has that happened? Have you worried about being fired, and how many times has that happened? Have you worried about your vacations being a total disaster, and how many times has that happened?

Your Doubts about Probabilities

Typically, people have several doubtful responses when asked to reconsider the probabilities in this way. However, these doubts only keep the worry going. The following are the most typical doubts:

"Even though it hasn't happened in the past, it could still happen." This type of thinking is one of the reasons why repeated disconfirmation (repeated

evidence to the contrary) does not change worrying. For example, Joan may have worried about being fired every day for the past six months, despite the fact that no one has ever told her that she makes too many mistakes, and even though her boss has always given her positive reviews. Why haven't these disconfirming pieces of evidence prevented Joan from worrying about the possibility of being fired? Most likely, it's because she continues to tell herself that, "There is always a first time, and today could be the day."

By believing that "it could still happen," you have thrown out all of the evidence and assumed that the probability of the negative event is high, without any valid reason. By telling yourself that the chance of being run over by a car when crossing the road is one in a million, but today could be that one in a million chance, mentally, you have inflated the chances of yourself being hit for no good reason.

"Negative events have not happened yet because I have always managed to prevent them. I always keep close watch on my children, I always make sure I get everything done on time, and I am always early for my appointments." As another example, you might think, "The reason why my neighbors have not rejected me is because my house is always clean." These examples represent the mistaken thought that your worry and anxious behaviors have actually prevented negative events.

Instead of realizing that the negative event is probably not going to happen, the tendency is to assume that the only reason why negative events have not occurred is because of your extra care and worry. Therefore, the extra behavioral cautions that you take convince you that negative events are very likely and must be prevented. In other words, your careful and safety-checking behaviors interfere with learning that your worries may not reflect the true situation. At the very least, you must realize that you do not know what the real risk is because you have never allowed the situation to arise (because you have always taken extra care to ensure that it does not). You can discover the real risks by testing what happens when you do not carry out your usual anxious, safety-checking behaviors. For example, you could test what happens if you do not clean your house before inviting a guest over, or what happens if you arrive exactly on time, or even a little late, for an appointment. This is the focus of chapter 9.

"But I have had bad things happen to me before, and I don't want anything like that to happen again, so by worrying, I can prepare myself for the worst and be ready for it." When a negative event has indeed happened (maybe you were fired, or maybe a family member came down with an illness, or

maybe your decision about a new car yielded more problems than you expected), it is important to return to probabilities and ways of coping. First, the fact that a negative event has happened does not necessarily mean that your chances of it happening again, or of other negative events happening, have increased. It is important to realize that negative events happen to everyone, and worrying will not necessarily prevent them from happening to you. Instead, focus on ways of coping when they do occur.

"Because I think about my children being kidnapped, then they could be kidnapped." This is called "thought-action fusion," or the tendency to confuse a thought with reality. Obviously, every day, we have many thoughts about different possibilities and events. The occurrence of these thoughts does not mean that they are important or that they will influence what actually happens.

What Are the Real Odds?

The first strategy for dealing with overestimation is to question the evidence for probability judgments. The general format for this strategy is to remind yourself that your thoughts are guesses, not facts, and that your interpretations represent one of many possible interpretations of given object or event. Next, question the evidence for a probability judgment. This involves asking the following questions: What are the real odds of this happening? Has this ever happened before? What is the evidence to suggest that it will not happen? For example, what are the real odds that my neighbors will think I am a slob if my house is not perfectly clean?

Consider all of the facts and evidence before making a prediction about the likelihood of an event. For example, you may think that your boss is upset with you because he did not greet you this morning, and fail to take into account your boss's own stresses. Similarly, you may assume that making a single mistake is catastrophic, and fail to realize that almost everyone makes mistakes occasionally.

Consider whether you are making negative predictions on the basis of a very limited set of past examples. For example, you may assume that you will be criticized for your performance on a particular task at work, when in the past, the reviews of your work were generally positive.

Consider whether you are confusing low probabilities with high probabilities, or acting and feeling as if negative outcomes are certainties, rather than possibilities. Remember, you may be able to list an array of possible negative outcomes, but that does not mean that those outcomes will come true.

The second strategy is to generate alternative interpretations that are based on facts and evidence. Use a pie chart to show alternative interpretations for your particular overestimation. Generate as many interpretations as you can, listing your one initial negative interpretation as one piece of the pie chart, as in the following example, which shows alternative interpretations regarding buying a new car.

Now, after considering the facts and considering alternative explanations or possibilities (using a pie chart), for the three to four examples from your Worry Records over the past couple of weeks, rate the probability of your initial negative interpretation on a 0- to 100-point scale (0 = it will never happen; 100 = it will definitely happen).

The third strategy for countering probability overestimates is to conduct mini-experiments that will gather data and provide evidence that disconfirms your misappraisals. Experiments are designed in such a way that spe-

Pie Chart Example

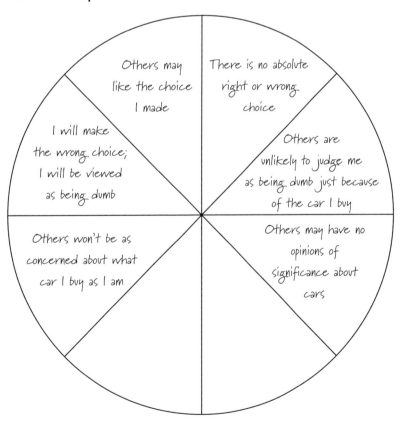

Pie Chart

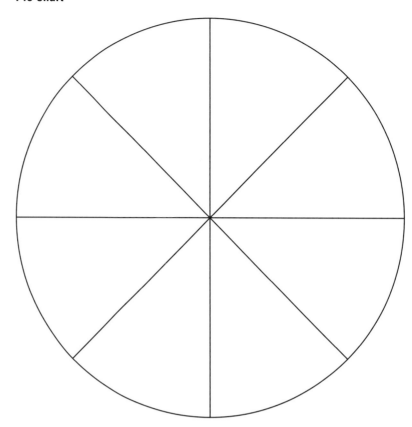

cific outcomes can be tested by the results. It is easiest to use extra-cautious behaviors as a way of testing hypotheses. For example, if you typically call your spouse twice a day to check his or her safety, then the hypothesis to be tested is whether he or she is safe, even if you call only once a day; or if you typically avoid looking your boss in the eye for fear of being reprimanded, then the hypothesis to test is whether you are reprimanded if you look at him directly. The hypothesis being tested is *not* related to the level of emotional distress in a situation (such as how anxious you will feel when you establish eye contact with your boss), but is about independent outcomes (such as the likelihood of being reprimanded). We will be focusing on these mini-experiments in chapter 9.

Homework

✎ Continue to practice relaxation.

✎ Continue keeping records of your daily mood and anxiety episodes.

✎ Challenge your anxious thoughts. For every episode of anxiety, identify your specific thoughts, evaluate the evidence, and consider the alternatives (using pie charts), and then rate the realistic probability using a 0- to 100-point scale.

✎ Begin using the Worry Record—Real Odds form. As shown in the following example, this new form includes a place to list alternatives to your worries and to rate the realistic probability that your worries will come true.

Worry Record—Real Odds Example

Date: _Tuesday 22nd_   Time began: _3:30_   (A.M. (P.M.)   Time ended: _8:00_   (A.M. (P.M.)

Maximum level of anxiety (circle a number below):

0 ----- 10 ----- 20 ----- 30 ----- 40 ----- 50 ----- 60 --- (70) --- 80 ----- 90 ----- 100

    None   Mild   Moderate   Strong   Extreme

Indicate which of the following symptoms you are experiencing:

Restlessness, feeling keyed up or on edge	✓
Easily fatigued	
Difficulty concentrating or mind going blank	✓
Irritability	✓
Muscle tension	✓
Sleep disturbance	

Triggering events: _Given a job to finish by end of work day_

Anxious thoughts: _won't finish in time, fired from job_

Real odds 0–100 _5_

Alternative possibilities: _I usually get things done & even if I don't get it finished, chances are low that I would be fired just for this_

Anxious behaviors: _Irritable, called home and told husband I would be late_

Worry Record—Real Odds

Date: _____   Time began: _____ (A.M./P.M.)   Time ended: _____ (A.M./P.M.)

Maximum level of anxiety (circle a number below):

0 ----- 10 ----- 20 ----- 30 ----- 40 ----- 50 ----- 60 ----- 70 ----- 80 ----- 90 ----- 100

None   Mild   Moderate   Strong   Extreme

Indicate which of the following symptoms you are experiencing:

Restlessness, feeling keyed up or on edge   _____

Easily fatigued   _____

Difficulty concentrating or mind going blank   _____

Irritability   _____

Muscle tension   _____

Sleep disturbance   _____

Triggering events: _____

_____

Anxious thoughts: _____

_____

Real odds 0–100 _____

Alternative possibilities: _____

_____

Anxious behaviors: _____

_____

Answer each of the following questions by circling T (true) or F (false). Answers are given in the appendix.

1. Two typical errors that people often make while they are anxious are called "overestimating the risk" and "catastrophizing."   T   F

2. It is very important to identify the specific predictions that you make when you are anxious.   T   F

3. Thoughts that tend to occur automatically can never be changed.   T   F

4. Avoiding worrisome thoughts is the most useful method for becoming less anxious.   T   F

5. To challenge overestimations, it is important to question the evidence and rate the realistic probability using a 0- to 100-point scale.   T   F

Chapter 7

Controlling Thoughts That Cause Anxiety: II. Thinking the Worst

Goals

- To review your records from the previous week and add data to your Progress Record

- To learn the recall-relaxation technique

- To understand the concepts of catastrophizing and decatastrophizing

- To begin using the Worry Record–Real Odds & Coping form

- To continue record-keeping

- To complete the self-assessment

Review of Your Records

Review your ratings on the Worry Record and the Daily Mood Record. What was your average level of maximum anxiety over the last week? Are you able to objectively describe the kind of anxiety that you experience? As a check, describe for yourself your most common anxious behaviors, physical symptoms and thoughts, and triggers, as well as the themes of your worries. Add the number of anxiety episodes per week and your average maximum anxiety ratings to your Progress Record. Has the number of episodes of anxiety increased or decreased? Think of possible reasons for the observed changes. In particular, if the number of anxious episodes or the level of maximum of anxiety has decreased, think of changes in your level of physical tension or your thoughts or behaviors that may have contributed to such decreases. Were there any events that you responded to differently than you would have responded before, and if so, what was different? For example, was a worry about the well-being of your family easier to dismiss because you recognized that you were overestimating the risk? Becoming aware of the reasons for changes in your anxiety level will help you to know what to concentrate on as you continue with the program.

Did you keep records of your anxious thoughts, the evidence, and the realistic probability for every anxiety episode that occurred? Were you able to identify your thoughts as specifically as possible by continuing to ask yourself questions until you reached the bottom line, or your most feared negative event? If not, do so now. For each bottom line feared negative event, think of all of the evidence available for and against its probability, consider alternative possibilities using a pie chart, and then rate the realistic probability using a 0- to 100-point scale. Remember, thinking or feeling that a particular event might happen does not count as evidence. Using thoughts and feelings as evidence is a common error. Do not base your 0- to 100-point rating on what you feel, but instead, base it on the evidence. We will spend more time discussing self-statements in this chapter.

Did you practice your relaxation exercise? Did you keep track of your levels of relaxation and concentration on the Relaxation Record? If you did not practice, think of reasons why and make corrections for the coming week. Remember, the benefit that you will receive from these exercises is based on how much you practice.

Relaxation

By this time, you should be regularly practicing the sixteen-muscle-group procedure, as well as either the eight- or the four-muscle-group procedure. If your relaxation ratings are below 50, or if your concentration levels are low, consider what could account for your difficulty. As we described in the previous chapters, typical reasons for low relaxation ratings are interruptions, fatigue, treating the relaxation exercise as a burden, trying too hard to relax, and an inadequate amount of time for relaxation because of the sense that there are too many other things to do. One of the benefits of relaxation training is that, by allowing yourself to let go of all other responsibilities and worries for a short period, you will learn to physically relax. You will also learn that some of the things that you believe must get done right now can actually wait, and also that relaxation does not lead to more negative events.

If you have successfully mastered the four-muscle-group procedure, it is time to move on to recall-relaxation. Instead of tensing the muscles before relaxing them, you will now relax the muscles simply through the power of concentration and recall. For the four major muscle groups that you have targeted up until now (probably the abdomen, chest, shoulders, and forehead), concentrate on each one in turn, and let the tension go as you think about what it feels like to relax each particular area of your body. As you breathe out, think the word "relax," and let go of the tension in each of the four major muscle groups. As you concentrate on your abdomen, think of your stomach muscles letting go, and feel the warmth of relaxation as your abdomen relaxes. As you concentrate on your chest, feel the air move in and out smoothly, as you inhale and exhale. Think about your shoulders, and as you let them droop, think of the sense of release from tension and the warmth and comfort of relaxation. Similarly, as you concentrate on your forehead, think about the feeling of release from tension as you smooth out the wrinkles. Allow yourself approximately five minutes to concentrate and relax while maintaining a pattern of slow, regular breathing, repeating the word "relax" silently to yourself each time you exhale. Continue to repeat the word "relax" as you exhale, to instill a sense of relaxation. This will be your exercise for the next week. For the moment, continue to practice this procedure in a quiet, comfortable location. Soon, you will move on to relaxing in more distracting and uncomfortable locations, so that relaxation becomes a portable skill or one that you could apply almost any, time in a variety of situations.

Recall-Relaxation Procedure

1. Pick a quiet location, such as a comfortable chair or bed.

2. Loosen tight clothing, and remove glasses or contact lenses.

3. Concentrate on each of the four muscle groups in turn: abdomen, chest, shoulders, and forehead.

4. Let go of the tension, as you recall the feelings of relaxation in each muscle group.

5. Relax for five minutes, maintaining a pattern of slow, regular breathing and repeating the word "relax" with every exhalation.

Perhaps you have tried to use the relaxation procedure at a time when you felt anxious, and became frustrated with it, or with yourself, because it didn't work. Because you are still learning to use relaxation, it is likely that it may not work well in more difficult situations. To expect to use relaxation effectively at times of high anxiety at this point would be the same as asking a pilot to make an emergency landing without having practiced all of the emergency procedures. Training is essential, and training in more and more difficult situations will occur over the next few weeks.

Thinking the Worst

Catastrophizing

Earlier, we talked about the basic principles of self-statements and introduced the notion of overestimating the risk, or assuming that negative events are very likely to happen, when in fact, the real probability is low. Overestimating the likelihood of a negative event increases anxiety, because anxiety is a response to the perception of threat or of negative events. We discussed the various ways in which overestimating the risk can continue, despite disconfirming evidence (see the section in chapter 6 that refers to "your doubts about probabilities"). If you do not recall the information from the last chapter, or are confused about the concept of overestimating the risk and how to correct it by questioning the real odds, we recommend that you reread the previous chapter before continuing.

In addition to overestimating the risk, anxiety is associated with a tendency to view impending events with a sense of catastrophe or disaster. "Catastrophizing" means blowing things out of proportion, or thinking the worst. Statements such as, "That would be terrible," "I could not live through that," or "I could never cope with that," give a sense of being unable to cope. Catastrophizing can occur while you are thinking about events that are likely to happen or events that are unlikely to happen. For example, one might catastrophize about others noticing a particular symptom of distress or anxiety that is indeed noticeable, such as blushing or trembling. An example might be, "They will think I'm really weak and incompetent. I would never be able to face them again." This is an example of catastrophizing an event that is likely— a visible symptom of anxiety. Or, one might catastrophize about others noticing a particular symptom of distress or anxiety that is not really noticeable at all, such as an upset stomach. An example might be, "They will know how bad I'm feeling and how uncomfortable my stomach feels, and they'll think I'm a real idiot." This is an example of catastrophizing an unlikely event.

Another type of catastrophizing is jumping to an extreme conclusion from an unimportant event. Some examples are, "If my house is not in perfect order, then I am no good," "If my children argue with each other, then it must mean that I have failed as a parent," and "If I make a mistake at work, then I am not right for this position." This type of catastrophizing is particularly relevant for those who find themselves striving for perfection and worrying about issues of responsibility. Remember, as we described earlier, thoughts such as, "Everything has to proceed in the right way, or something bad might happen," "I must get everything finished on time," and "if I don't worry, then something really could go wrong," result from underlying beliefs that: (1) negative events are indeed very likely, (2) worrying prevents those events from happening, and (3) since you can predict what those events might be, it is your responsibility to be worried and to prevent their occurrence, because failure to do so means that you are neglecting your responsibilities. Through self-statement training, we aim to shift the perception that negative events are likely to occur at any moment, to help you to realize that worrying has no effect on the probability of independent events, and to help you to learn that letting go of worries does not mean that you are irresponsible, because what you are worried about is unlikely to occur in the first place. Responsibility is important only when the event that you are worried about is of high probability. Most of the events that concern people who worry chronically are of low probability. Another underlying belief has to do with a sense of incompetence, or the notion that, "If I make a mistake in my decisions or judgments, then I am incompetent." Sometimes this idea is related to a concern that other respected individuals will recognize our mistakes, whether that person is our boss, a parent, a friend, or a spouse. It is important to recognize that everyone makes mistakes, and in most cases, you are likely overestimating the significance of the mistake.

Decatastrophizing

Decatastrophizing involves imagining the worst possible outcome and then objectively judging its severity. Usually, you will realize that, although the event that you were worried about, if it were to come true, would be unpleasant, nonetheless, it would be manageable and time-limited. This means that you would be able to cope with the event and that the unpleasantness would not continue forever. Although some events may be very unpleasant, and you would not wish them on anyone (such as losing a loved one), the reality is that there is a way to survive these unpleasant events. It is important to recognize that there is a way to continue, even if the event brings about sadness and struggle. This is a more effective way of managing anxiety about such events than focusing on how horrible the event would be, without further consideration of ways to manage it. Recognizing your ability to cope with negative events involves recognizing alternative solutions to problems, as opposed to continuing to dwell on the catastrophic nature of negative outcomes. Thinking of a negative event as a disaster is very different from thinking of the same event with the realization that you can cope with it. We have to examine the evidence at hand to realize that we usually do cope, in one way or another, even when very negative events happen, such as wars, losing loved ones, or severe illnesses. In fact, great strength and mastery may come out of conditions of real sorrow or threat. This is not to say that all of the events that you worry about will occur. Decatastrophizing is just another strategy for learning to control the tendency to worry excessively about negative events. Decatastrophizing allows you to see that you can cope with negative outcomes that do occur.

Imagine yourself being reprimanded at work for having missed a very obvious mistake in a very important document that resulted in the firm losing a big project. Your boss is obviously disappointed in you. The question is how to manage the situation. The catastrophic approach would be to interpret this situation as a sign that you are incompetent in general, irresponsible in your decision-making, and out of control, and that this mistake represents the loss of all respect from others. The decatastrophizing approach would be to recognize that, while this is a very difficult situation that has had real consequences for your firm, everyone makes mistakes, and the severity of the situation will subside with time. In all likelihood, the people around you will continue to perceive you similarly to the way they perceived you before this event, and if even if they don't, that, too, will subside with time. To make a mistake is to be human, and to be judged negatively by others some of the time is part of everyone's existence.

In most cases, you can handle a worrisome thought by evaluating the evidence to consider the probabilities and by decatastrophizing. For example, let's say that you are worried about making mistakes at work and being fired as a result. You can challenge these thoughts by asking the following key questions: What is the likelihood that I will make a major mistake? What is the likelihood that my boss would fire me if I did make a mistake? And if I did get fired, what steps would I take to cope with the situation? For example, would you look for another job, seek assistance from friends or family, or take a break from work?

Review the episodes of anxiety that you recorded over the past couple of weeks, and evaluate whether any of your thoughts are examples of catastrophizing, or blowing things out of proportion. In other words, have you had the feeling that an event, if it were to happen, would be unmanageable or terrible?

For each episode of anxiety, question the assumption that the negative event would be a catastrophe. In some ways, you are being asked to say to yourself, "So what if it happens? I can deal with it." Of course, as discussed earlier, some situations are certainly negative, and it is not accurate to say, "It doesn't matter." However, it is important to realize that we all live through bad times, and even if negative events happen, life goes on and you can cope.

Putting Catastrophizing and Decatastrophizing Together

An example of catastrophizing and decatastrophizing with the help of a therapist follows:

Therapist: You said earlier that you sometimes worry again and again about the effect that your death would have on your family. Tell me more about this worry.

Sandra: Well, I worry because I don't want my kids to go through what I went through, and am still going through, when my father died last year. Besides the horrible sense of sadness they would suffer, who would look after them, and what would happen to them if I weren't around?

Therapist: What kind of situation do you imagine if you were to die? What would happen to your children?

Sandra: (Teary) It's really hard to talk about because I think it would be so terrible. I see them being alone, and crying, and not knowing what to do.

Therapist: These kinds of thoughts are obviously very distressing for you. Let's evaluate them. First of all, let's consider the possibility of overestimating the risk. Do you have any reason to believe that you'll die unexpectedly or soon?

Sandra:	Only that my father died suddenly.
Therapist:	What was the reason?
Sandra:	Apparently, he had a heart condition that we didn't know about.
Therapist:	What evidence do you have to believe that you have the same condition?
Sandra:	None, actually. I had a complete checkup a few months after he died because I was so worried, and I'm in fine shape.
Therapist:	Given the available evidence about your own health and the population statistic for a woman of your age dying unexpectedly for no apparent reason, what is the real probability of that you will die soon? Use the 0- to 100-point scale.
Sandra:	When I think of it that way, I suppose it's really low— maybe 10%.
Therapist:	So, you're telling me that for every day you live over the next few years, you have a one in ten chance of dying on any given day?
Sandra:	(Laugh) No, I guess it's lower than that, probably less than 1%.
Therapist:	Okay, now there are other areas where you seem to have made assumptions and overlooked the evidence. Can you think of any?
Sandra:	You mean the way my children would feel? I really believe that they would feel terrible.
Therapist:	No, I'm not questioning the sadness and loss, but I am questioning your assumption that their lives would continue in that way. Even though it's difficult to think about, imagine what would happen over time, after your death.
Sandra:	I suppose that, eventually, things would get back to some kind of normalcy, although not the same as if I were there. Their father is a good dad. He could probably look after them.
Therapist:	Again, I want to emphasize that we are not saying that you most likely will die in the near future, or that you should think about it with a carefree attitude. However, realizing that, as difficult as it would be for them to lose you, your children

may be able to survive and continue without you. That's a very different way of looking at the situation. Do you agree?

Sandra: Yes, I understand. I think I tend to do that with a lot of things. I think of the worst and just focus on that, without considering the alternatives.

Notice how this example demonstrates that negative thoughts can become so powerful that reasonable alternatives aren't even considered. Sandra hadn't considered the possibility of her family coping without her; she had only considered how terrible it would be if she were to die. It is important that you give full consideration to alternative ways of coping with future negative events or problems, so that you can interrupt the tendency to worry chronically, without ever reaching a solution or recognizing an alternative. Take the earlier example of worrying about being fired. Even though the probability of being fired may be low, it is important to realize that losing one's job does not have to mean a catastrophe. Looking for another job may not be enjoyable, but it can be done. Another example is the feeling of being overwhelmed and not having enough time to get tasks done. A good way to interrupt this worrisome thought is to ask yourself, What's the worst that can happen? For example, "What's the worst that can happen if I don't get everything done by the end of the day, or if somebody has to wait until tomorrow? So what if I leave the office without tidying my desk, or leave the house without making sure that it's in perfect order! What's the worst that can happen if I take thirty minutes to relax?" Your response might be, "If I don't get everything done today, it will pile up tomorrow and continue to pile up forever." In reality, there will always be things to be done, and one can never really reach the point of having everything completed. A more effective strategy is to accept the fact that there will always be things to do and to realize they don't all have to get done immediately. In chapter 10, we describe ways to manage work overload.

Decatastrophizing Personal Examples

Go back to each example of catastrophic thinking that you recorded over the past couple of weeks. As objectively as you can, consider the meaning that you gave the event to see where you might be blowing things out of proportion, and where alternatives can be generated. Keep in mind that the goal of decatastrophizing is not positive thinking, but a realistic appraisal of possible outcomes.

Just as you used a pie chart to generate alternative interpretations for errors of overestimation, you can use a pie chart to generate alternative meanings of negative events. The following example shows alternative meanings of being fired.

It is important to remember that, decatastrophizing means placing events in perspective, and that means accepting the idea that we cannot prevent all negative events from happening, no matter how much we try. In addition, making mistakes is a normal part of human existence. The error is in blowing errors out of proportion by: (1) viewing mistakes as more significant than they really are, such as viewing our mistakes as a sign of a fatal character flaw or a sign of overall incompetence; and (2) failing to consider realistic ways of coping, should negative events occur.

Next, switch gears from focusing on "how bad it would be if it happened" to considering "ways of dealing with it." No matter how intense your fear,

Decatastrophizing Pie Chart Example

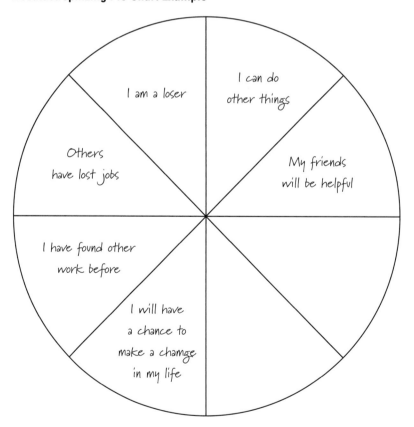

Decatastrophizing Pie Chart

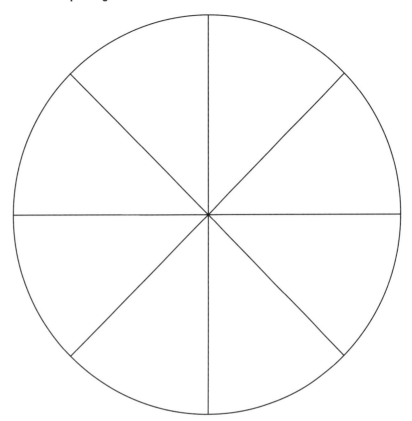

you will survive. No matter how distressing the moment, it will pass. So, the final step in decatastrophizing is to generate ways of coping with the event, if it were to happen. Think through what you would do if, for example, you received a negative review at work, lost your job, found out that you made the wrong choice when purchasing a car or house, or lost a child. Remember, you may become more anxious initially, as you face the situation and consider ways of coping, especially if you believe that the negative events are your responsibility. In these situations, the goal is to recognize that: (1) the event is unlikely to occur, (2) you are unlikely to be fully responsible for all negative events, (3) negative events happen to everyone, and (4) there are ways of coping with any event.

In fact, it is likely that, in the past, the intense anxiety associated with these thoughts led you to think desperately about something else, without fully addressing your main fear. For example, the anxiety associated with thinking about losing a loved one may lead you to divert your attention to other worries about less important things. Here, we are asking you to face directly the events that you are most afraid of, and by facing them directly, to realize that, as negative as they may be, there is a way to manage them. As we discuss in more detail in the next chapter, you will find that thoughts become less anxiety-provoking the more often you face them directly and consider ways to cope.

Worry Record—Real Odds & Coping Example

Date: _Friday 15th_   Time began: _10:00_   (A.M. (P.M.))   Time ended: _11:30_   (A.M. (P.M.))

Maximum level of anxiety (circle a number below):

0 ----- 10 ----- 20 ----- 30 ----- 40 ----- 50 ----- 60 ----- 70 ---(80)--- 90 ----- 100

   None   Mild   Moderate   Strong   Extreme

Indicate which of the following symptoms you are experiencing:

Restlessness, feeling keyed up or on edge	✓
Easily fatigued	
Difficulty concentrating or mind going blank	✓
Irritability	✓
Muscle tension	✓
Sleep disturbance	

Triggering events: _Daughter went out with her friends and has not called_

Anxious thoughts: _She was in a car accident and is injured and disoriented_

Real odds 0–100 _3_

Alternative possibilities: _She is having fun with her friends, she forgot to call, she will call later_

Ways of coping: _if she is injured, I will help her recover_

Anxious behaviors: _waited by the phone_

Worry Record—Real Odds & Coping

Date: _____ Time began: _____ (A.M./P.M.) Time ended: _____ (A.M./P.M.)

Maximum level of anxiety (circle a number below):

0 ----- 10 ----- 20 ---- 30 ----- 40 ----- 50 ----- 60 ----- 70 ----- 80 ----- 90 ----- 100

None   Mild   Moderate   Strong   Extreme

Indicate which of the following symptoms you are experiencing:

Restlessness, feeling keyed up or on edge   _____

Easily fatigued   _____

Difficulty concentrating or mind going blank   _____

Irritability   _____

Muscle tension   _____

Sleep disturbance   _____

Triggering events: _____

_____

Anxious thoughts: _____

_____

Real odds 0–100 _____

Alternative possibilities: _____

_____

Ways of coping: _____

_____

Anxious behaviors: _____

_____

Homework

✎ Continue your daily monitoring using the Worry Record and the Daily Mood Record.

✎ Practice relaxation and recording your ratings on the Relaxation Record.

✎ Use both types of strategies to counter anxious thoughts: (1) question the evidence, consider alternatives, and rate the realistic odds; and (2) consider the worst that can happen, consider alternatives, and think of ways to cope.

✎ Begin using the new Worry Record—Real Odds & Coping form. On this form, in addition to recording alternative possibilities and realistic odds of your worrisome thought coming true, you can record ways to cope with negative events.

Self-Assessment

Answer each of the following questions by circling T (true) or F (false). Answers are given in the appendix.

1. The best thing to do when I become anxious is to try to focus on something else.   T   F

2. Recall-relaxation means bringing on a state of relaxation through deep concentration and recalling the feelings of relaxation.   T   F

3. To decatastrophize means to face the worst and consider ways of coping.   T   F

4. Changing my thoughts is the same thing as positive thinking.   T   F

5. Questioning real evidence and evaluating coping resources are the ways to challenge anxious thoughts.   T   F

Chapter 8

Getting to the Heart of Worrying:
Facing Your Fears

Goals

▦ To review your records from the previous week and add data to your Progress Record

▦ To learn the cue-controlled relaxation technique

▦ To learn realistic thinking strategies

▦ To practice imagery exposure

▦ To continue record-keeping

▦ To complete the self-assessment

Review of Your Records

Review your records from the previous week, and add your data to your Progress Record. Did you monitor your thoughts every time you felt anxious, and were you able to question the evidence and evaluate your ability to cope with negative events? If you have not done so, spend the next week closely monitoring and challenging your thoughts. As mentioned earlier, this program proceeds in a sequence, so that each new step depends on the steps learned earlier. It is essential that you have a good grasp of overestimating the risk and catastrophizing (thinking the worst) in relation to your own thinking. Actively challenging your thoughts takes some effort and may feel artificial initially, but practice helps to develop a stronger, realistic thinking style. As we described before, one of the reasons why anxious worries come to mind so often is because they have become habitual, or automatic, through repetition. For the alternative, realistic styles of thinking, to become habitual, you must practice and rehearse them, just as you would if you were studying a new language. With repetition, the new alternatives will become the more natural approach, and then you will no longer need to work at changing your anxious thoughts. It will happen naturally.

Relaxation

If you are successful with the four-muscle-group recall relaxation procedure (that is, you can achieve at least a moderate level of relaxation through concentration and regular breathing for approximately five minutes), it is time to move on to one-step relaxation. It's okay if you need more practice with the four-muscle-group recall-relaxation procedure; just delay the new one-step procedure until next week.

The one-step procedure is called "cue-controlled relaxation," and it is based on all of the relaxation practice you have done up until now, specifically, all of the times that you have paired the word "relax" with a feeling of relaxation. Now, we will use the word "relax" to bring on the feelings of relaxation. With the one-step procedure, you take a few slow breaths, and when breathing out, you repeat the word "relax" to yourself, while letting your whole body relax. Do not take unusually deep breaths; take slow, smooth breaths. As you exhale, let go of all of the tension in your body and relax into a drooping position. Practice taking four or five breathes and repeating the word "relax" on each exhalation, as you release the tension from your body. Concentrate on the feelings of relaxation.

Cue-Controlled Relaxation Procedure

1. When you notice tension, focus on your body and take four to five slow, smooth breaths.

2. On each exhalation, repeat the word "relax" to yourself.

3. Release the tension in your body with each exhalation.

4. Concentrate on the feelings of relaxation.

5. Maintain a pattern of slow, regular breathing.

6. Practice this one-step procedure in a variety of situations, such as at home, at work, while driving in traffic, and while waiting in line.

7. Use this technique multiple times throughout the day, in as many different situations as possible.

For the rest of the week, practice the cue-controlled procedure several times a day in various locations, not just in quiet, peaceful locations. The training phase is almost over, and as a last step, it is important to extend your practice to situations that are not truly conducive to relaxation. This will be a test of your ability to concentrate as well, since relaxing in the presence of other noises and people means cutting yourself off from the things around you, just to concentrate on relaxing. Practice cue-controlled relaxation at home, while waiting at traffic lights, at your desk, or in a movie theater. Practice as much as you can. You need a week of solid practice in as many situations as you can. From now on, it is no longer necessary to monitor your relaxation using the Relaxation Record.

Facing Your Fears: Taking the Bite out of Worry

Up until now, the goal has been to learn ways to control worrisome thoughts when they arise. Now the goal is to deliberately face the negative images that underlie the worry and learn to be less affected by them. As we described in chapter 2, there is evidence to show that much worrisome thinking is driven by images or pictures in one's mind of catastrophic events, as if they were actually happening. For example, if your worries are about your children's safety, then it is possible that these worries are connected to a picture or an image of your children being injured and you being blamed for being an irresponsible parent. The picture represents a visualization of the scene as if it were actually happening. Since this picture or image typically creates a high level of emotional distress and fear, it is not uncommon for people to divert their attention to worrying about checking on their children's safety, calling the school to make sure that the children are okay, and so forth. Such worry tends to be associated with less intense emotional distress than picturing catastrophic images, and therefore, becomes a preferred mode of operating. However, by avoiding the images through worrying, the images are likely to occur again. Now, it is time to face the fear and learn not to be afraid so that you don't have to worry so much. We know that fear will decrease through exposure, and so our goal in this chapter is to practice repeated exposure to the most feared images, while you are encouraged to think about what would happen as the feared image unfolds, and to do so repeatedly until the fear decreases.

You will need to identify the most frightening, catastrophic image at the end of your chain of worries by asking yourself, "What is the worst-case scenario?" This is an extension of the work you did in the last chapter on identifying catastrophic thinking, but now you are going to focus on images, or pictures in your mind, rather than verbal statements of things that you worry about. The most frightening images are those brief pictures that pop into your mind that involve extreme catastrophe, such as a family member dying, being homeless and living on the streets, or being humiliated in front of your entire firm. You will identify the catastrophic image associated with each of your main topics of worry—your family, job security, health, and so on. For each worry, generate a description of the image that is tied to the worry in as much detail as possible, as if it were actually happening. Describe the situation that you imagine; your physical responses of fear, such as feeling sick to your stomach, a racing heart, or shortness of breath; and the meaning that you give to the situation, such as, "I am a sham and a failure." An example of an image in descriptive form would be, "Upon my yearly evaluation, my boss told me that my work was not up to par, and that I am too slow and make too many mistakes. I was fired and can no longer afford my apartment. I cannot find anywhere else to live. I am living on the streets. I feel weak, fragile, and disoriented. I believe that this has happened because I screwed up and that I am incompetent." Use the following Imagery Description form to help generate images for each main topic of your worry. Again, for each image, describe the situation, your physical responses, and the meaning you give to the situation. Spaces for three different images are provided, but you may add more, if necessary.

Now that you have generated several images, rate each one from 0 to 100 in terms of the level of distress that each one evokes as you think about what you have written. By facing these images repeatedly, you will learn something new. Specifically, you will learn that the emotional distress will decrease with repeated exposure, and that the image is just that, an image. In other words, repeated exposure to the image will enable you to change the meaning that you give to the image. For example, an image of a car accident is distressing only if you believe that the image means that the car accident is actually going to happen or that it is a result of your own incompetence. By imagining the scene repeatedly, you will learn that the image does not represent reality. In addition, facing your feared images and asking yourself how events will unfold after the worst-case scenario happens

Imagery Description

Image 1:

    Situation: _____

_____

_____

    Fear responses: _____

_____

_____

    Meaning: _____

_____

_____

Image 2:

    Situation: _____

_____

_____

    Fear responses: _____

_____

_____

    Meaning: _____

_____

_____

Image 3:

    Situation: _____

_____

_____

    Fear responses: _____

_____

_____

    Meaning: _____

_____

_____

will enable you to think about realistic odds and ways of coping, using the tools you have already mastered. For example, if your feared image is of losing your job, the imagery exposure encourages you not only to imagine this event, but also to imagine what would happen after the event. For example, you will be encouraged to imagine what will happen one week, six months, and one year later.

Imagery Training

For imagery exposure, it is essential that you imagine the worse event happening and concentrate on it as hard as you can. Do not avoid the image, since avoiding it will defeat the purpose of the exercise. The skill of imagining can be practiced by first using pleasant scenes that do not involve anxiety. Imagine as best you can by putting yourself in a situation, not as if you are watching it like a movie, but as if you are really there. In other words, see the things and people around you, hear the sounds, and experience the situation physically and emotionally. Practice the technique by imagining the pleasant scenarios listed below. To do this, you may record each of the scenes on an audiotape, and then close your eyes while you play the tape and imagine the scene as vividly as you can. Repeat this procedure two or three times, remembering to focus on the physical experiences as you imagine.

Imagery Scene 1

You are sitting by a window. The window is square, with one clear pane of glass. There are yellow and white checkered curtains on the side. You are sitting on a soft chair, and you feel comfortable and relaxed. Your elbows are on the windowsill, and your hands are clasped under your chin. The sun is streaming in through the window, onto your face and hands. You feel warm, and the light is bright. You close your eyes and feel the warm sun.

Imagery Scene 2

You walk into a square room. The walls and ceiling are all a deep blue. On the floor is a blue carpet. The carpet is soft under your bare feet. There is nothing in the room, except for a plain wooden table in the middle. On the table, you see a clear glass pitcher filled with water and a tall, clear glass filled with ice. You are thirsty, and you are glad to see the water. Your mouth is very dry. You walk over to the table and pick up the pitcher in one hand and the glass in the other. You fill the glass with water. The hand that holds the glass feels cool as you fill the glass with water. You put the pitcher back on the table, and take a sip from the glass, letting the cold water flow slowly down your throat. You continue to drink the cold water and feel the sensation of water quenching your thirst.

Imagery Scene 3

It is summer. You are walking up a hill. You are on a dirt path lined with lilies. The lilies are bright yellow. You can smell them in the wind. The day is hot, and your feet feel tired. The ground is soft and not easy to walk on. You begin to sweat a little bit, and you rub your forehead with the back of your hand. The back of your hand feels wet. You get close to the top of the hill, and you begin to hurry. You can feel your heart pound as you reach the top. At the top is a soft patch of grass, in the shade, under a tree. You sit down on the grass and rest. You look at the path with the yellow lilies.

As you can see, each of these images is filled with sensations. As you imagine your own fearful images, incorporate fear responses (i.e., fear sensations), along with a description of the situation and the meaning that you give the situation. Once you have practiced imagery scenes several times, you will be ready to begin the actual exposure.

Procedures for Imagery Exposure

A specific set of procedures is to be used for the imagery exposure. Remember, follow these procedures after you have practiced with the pleasant imagery scenes.

1. Begin with the image associated with the least distress. Read your description, and then sit back, close your eyes, and imagine the scene as if it were actually happening. For example, the image might be of your spouse lying unconscious, and slumped over the steering wheel of a car. You are in the image as well. You feel weak and sick to your stomach, and you are about to faint. The meaning that you give to

this imagined scenario is that you are to blame, and that you should have known better than to let him or her drive home late after work. Again, imagine the scene as if it is actually happening, and include the situation, your fear response sensations, and the meaning you give to the situation in the imagery.

2. After about 30 seconds, rate the vividness, or clarity, of the image and the maximum level of anxiety that you experience, using a 0- to 100-point scale, where 0 equals no image and no anxiety and 100 equals an extremely vivid image and extreme anxiety. An example of these ratings is on the Exposure Record.

3. If the image is not clear or is rated less than 50 on the 0- to 100-point scale of vividness, spend another minute or so imagining the event. Remember to imagine yourself in the setting, not as an observer, but as a participant, and focus on the different fear response sensations and emotions that you imagine experiencing. If the image remains vague, practice several more times with the pleasant scenes described earlier. It is possible that your imagery is not clear because the particular image that you chose was not very frightening. If this is the case, choose the next most distressing image on your list. It is also possible that the image is not clear because it is too frightening and your mind is preventing you from letting yourself really experience what it is you fear. If this is the case, then continue with the exposure to this image, with the reassurance that the image, is just an image, and that by focusing on it, you are not causing the frightening scene to come true.

4. Once you have achieved a vivid image that is emotionally evocative, meaning that it produces some anxiety, the goal is to observe the image mindfully for five minutes. This may require repeated reading of the description of the image on your Imagery Description Form. After you read the description, close your eyes and imagine the event, as if it were actually happening. You might set a timer to let you know when the five-minute period is up. As you imagine the event, let yourself experience whatever emotions are actually produced by the image. Do not attempt to change either the image or your emotional experience. At this stage, the most important thing is to let yourself face the image and the associated emotions. As a result of repeated exposure to the image, the distress that it evokes and the

meaning that you ascribe to it will change. If your mind wanders during the five-minute interval, simply redirect your attention to the imagined situation, the imagined emotional and physical response, and the imagined meaning that you give to the situation, and again, let yourself observe the image and experience whatever emotions are produced by the image.

5. After you complete five minutes of imagery, shift your attention to cue-controlled relaxation by taking several slow abdominal breaths, repeating the word "relax" to yourself on each exhalation, and letting your body relax into a drooped position. Then, ask yourself the following questions about the image: Because I imagined this event, will it come true? If this imagined event were to occur, what would I do to cope? Where am I overmagnifying the meaning of this imagined event? What is the realistic likelihood of this imagined event occurring? By asking these questions, your goal is to develop more realistic interpretations and coping solutions for the imagined event, recognizing all the while that it is just an image.

6. Once you have completed the relaxation procedure and answered the questions, repeat the entire imagining exercise. Read the description, and then imagine the event, as if it were actually happening, for about 30 seconds. Rate the vividness of the image and the level of anxiety associated with the image. When you have a vivid image that is associated with at least some anxiety, continue imagining for five minutes, but this time, imagine not only the event, but also what would happen the next day, the next week, or the next month. In other words, imagine yourself actually coping with the imagined event. For example, see yourself one week after having lost your job, and then one month later. Then, practice cue-controlled relaxation and questioning of your self-statements, using the questions listed earlier. You might find that, as your emotional distress in response to the image decreases, your ability to imagine also decreases. This is to be expected, since the vividness of the imagery is partly due to its emotional intensity. The more you practice exposure to the image, the less frightening it will become, and hence, the less vivid it will be.

7. Continue for the number of repetitions necessary for your level of anxiety to decrease to 25 or less on the 0- to 100-point scale. Then, move to the next distressing image on your list, and begin the procedure again.

Exposure Record Example

Date	Image Description (key words)	Vividness 0–100	Maximum Anxiety 0–100
Monday 5th	Husband dead	95	85
Tuesday 6th	Husband dead	90	70
Wednesday 7th	Husband dead	80	40
Thursday 8th	Husband dead	70	20
Friday 9th	Living on streets	90	80
Saturday 10th	Living on streets	80	40
Monday 12th	Living on streets	70	25

We recommend that you practice the imagery exposure each day (3 times, 5 minutes each) for the next week or two. Do not go on to the next chapter until you have completed one or two weeks of imagery exposure.

Potential Difficulties with Imagery Exposure

The following is a list of potential difficulties that you might encounter with imagery exposure, some of which we described in the previous section.

1. Sometimes it is difficult to fully and vividly imagine the worst-case scenario because you fear the image, because you are unskilled in imagining, or because you have chosen an image that is not sufficiently anxiety-producing. If you are afraid to imagine a particular scenario, remember not to confuse images with facts. Deliberately inducing a fearful image does not mean that the imagined event will come true. Also, remember that, with repetition, the distress that you feel will decrease. If you are having trouble imagining in general, practice with the pleasant scenes, focusing on the different sensations associated with each scene. If the image does not develop because it does not produce enough distress, then find another image that elicits more anxiety or distress.

2. Sometimes the procedure is not effective because the image is too general. Be as specific as you can in the images that come to mind.

Exposure Record

Date	Image Description (key words)	Vividness 0–100	Maximum Anxiety 0–100

For example, if the image is the "future," you can make it more specific by imagining that five years from now you are unemployed, have no money, lose your house, and so on.

3. Sometimes images produce little or no anxiety. This can occur if the image is not vivid (vividness will come with practice and willingness to experience distress) or because the procedure has immediately helped you to view your concern more objectively. That is, by telling yourself to face the catastrophic images directly, you already may be recognizing that the image represents events that are unlikely to occur, or that could be managed if they did occur, or that the image is just an image. If so, then you have accomplished what you need to accomplish with the specific image, and you may move on to the next one. However, be absolutely sure that you are not just avoiding an image that distresses you.

4. Another potential difficulty is that you may experience little or no decrease in emotional distress with repetition of the imagery. This can happen if the image continuously changes. Remember to repeat the same image until your distress decreases, and then move on to the next image.

5. Finally, sometimes you will find that writing out or recording the images, as outlined earlier, is simply not enough to create emotional distress. Sometimes a real-life trigger is required, such as reading stories in newspapers and magazines about death, car accidents, robberies, and so on. Newspapers are full of this type of information, and for this reason, you may have learned to avoid them because they make you anxious. Now, it is time to overcome that fear. Look for newspaper stories that relate to your own catastrophic images, and use them to develop images of the catastrophic events you fear.

Homework

✎ Practice cue-controlled relaxation whenever and wherever you can.

✎ Apply realistic thinking strategies by considering the real odds, alternative possibilities, and ways of coping for each worrisome thought.

✎ Practice the imagery exposure exercise at least once a day, using three images of five minutes each, with the second and third five-minute image extending to visualizing yourself one day later, one week later, one month later, and so on, beyond the time of the imagined event, for the next week. Record your practice using the Exposure Record.

✎ Continue to use the Worry Record and the Daily Mood Record.

Self-Assessment

Answer each of the following questions by circling T (true) or F (false). Answers are given in the appendix.

1. Imagining the worse outcome of your worries should be avoided at all costs.   T   F

2. It is best to keep as calm as possible while facing your feared images directly.   T   F

3. You should use relaxation and realistic thinking after you generate the image and not while you are imagining.   T   F

4. Imagining a catastrophic event will increase your naturally occurring worries.   T   F

5. Cue-controlled relaxation should be done at the same time and in the same place every day.   T   F

Chapter 9　From Fears to Behaviors

Goals

- To review your records from the previous week and add data to your Progress Record

- To learn to apply cue-controlled relaxation whenever you feel anxious

- To fill out the Anxious Behaviors form

- To record your progress on the Behavioral Change form

- To continue record-keeping

- To complete the self-assessment

Review of Your Records

You should have spent the last one to two weeks practicing exposure to images, interspersed with cue-controlled relaxation and realistic thinking strategies (questioning the real odds, considering alternatives, and generating ways of coping). Add your summary data to your Progress Record. Examine the patterns that you have observed since the beginning of the program. It is possible that the imagery exposure practices over the last couple of weeks have increased your level of anxiety or the number of episodes of anxiety, because you have been focusing on the very things that frighten you most. However, this initial increase in anxiety will decrease. The more comfortable you become with the images, realizing that they are just images, the less anxiety you will experience.

Did you practice cue-controlled relaxation in as many different situations as possible? This particular relaxation exercise will not work if you have been getting upset about not relaxing right away. Nor will it work if you believe that you must relax completely or things will be a disaster. If you feel desperate every time you try to relax, it's almost guaranteed that you will not be able to relax. Remember, relaxation is a useful strategy for calming yourself, but it is not necessary for your survival. The next, and final step, in relaxation training is to use this tool throughout the day, as you feel tension or anxiety building. Up until now, you have been using these methods in either relaxing situations or distracting environments. The final phase is to apply cue-controlled relaxation whenever tension builds. As you feel your muscle tension increasing, whether you are at work, in the car, or trying to get the kids ready for bed, take a few slow, abdominal breaths, repeat to yourself the word "relax" on each exhalation, and physically let go of the tension in your body. This brief interruption of the cycle of anxiety and tension may be very effective in helping you to gain a different perspective on whatever it is you're dealing with at that moment. In fact, each time you notice anxiety and tension building, first, relax using the cue-controlled procedure; and then ask yourself these questions: What it is that I'm worried about? What are the real odds of that happening? What is the worst that can happen? How would I cope with that if it were to come true?

Imagery Exposure

Follow the procedure described in the last chapter for any remaining images on your list. As a reminder, the method is to imagine the worst-case scenario, as if it were actually happening, including a description of the situation, your physical responses to the situation, and the meaning that you give to the situation. After about 30 seconds, rate the vividness and anxiety associated with the image. If the image is sufficiently vivid, imagine the scene, as if it were actually happening, for approximately five minutes. If your mind wanders during that time, just return your attention to the situation, your responses, and the meaning you give the situation. If it is difficult to imagine a scene vividly, go back to your Imagery Description Form and remind yourself of the scene, and then close your eyes and imagine it, as if it were happening. After five minutes, practice cue-controlled relaxation and then think through the questions that were posed in the last chapter: Because I imagined this event, will it come true? If this imagined event were to occur, what would I do to cope? Where am I overmagnifying the meaning of this imagined event? What is the realistic likelihood of this imagined event coming true? Then, repeat the imagery exposure for two more five-minute periods, each time imagining forward in time to visualize yourself coping beyond the point at which the imagined negative event occurred.

The goals of this exposure are to reduce the level of emotional distress in response to the image and to learn to reevaluate the significance of the image by recognizing that it is just an image, and that the imagined event is unlikely to occur, and that, if it were to occur, it would be manageable in some way.

Worry Behavior

The next step toward controlling your worry and anxiety involves work in everyday situations. From chapter 3, you may recall that we described anxious behaviors as behaviors that are designed to: (1) prevent bad things from happening, (2) prevent yourself from worrying, and (3) provide reassurance. Although these behaviors may seem small and insignificant, they can play a very big role in perpetuating anxiety and worry. If you continually use these types of behaviors to "keep yourself and your family safe," to minimize the likelihood of worrying, or to obtain reassurance, then you never give yourself the chance to learn that whatever you are worried about either may not happen, or if it were to happen, could be managed. In other words, these anxious behaviors reinforce worry. An example of an anxious behavior designed to prevent bad things from happening might be staying late at work every night so as not to be reprimanded the next day for not having completed everything that was assigned. An anxious behavior designed to prevent worry may be avoiding taking on extra responsibilities for fear that the responsibilities would cause you to worry. An anxious behavior designed to provide reassurance might be checking on the safety of family members throughout the day.

Of course, some safety-checking and avoidance behaviors are very important and worthwhile. If you are living in a dangerous neighborhood, it makes sense to be more concerned and to check more carefully on the safety of your children, for example. If a gang of delinquents is terrorizing the neighborhood, for example, it would be worthwhile to prevent your children from walking outside without the protection of an adult. However, if your neighborhood is safe, then it is not necessary to protect your children as much. Similarly, if your husband or wife is in good physical health, then it is not necessary to check on him or her regularly during the day. And, it is probably not necessary to make the extra effort to keep your house perfectly clean so as to prevent being judged negatively by unexpected visitors.

On the Anxious Behaviors form, make a list of all of the behaviors that you recognize as being excessive and based on worry. Use your Worry Records over the past few weeks to help you identify your most common anxious behaviors. Remember, anxious behaviors may take many forms, including checking or reassurance-seeking, saying "no" to additional demands or responsibilities for fear of becoming worried, overprotectiveness with regard to your family and making an extra effort at work for fear of being fired. An example of a completed form follows; notice that, for each anxious behavior, you will eventually list a nonanxious behavior, but leave that section of the form blank for now.

From this list of behaviors, you will develop a set of tasks that are designed to replace the anxious behaviors with nonanxious behaviors. As a specific example, if your anxious behavior is to always arrive early at appointments for fear of being late, then the task would be to arrive on time, instead of early. Similarly, if your anxious behavior is to check on your family members repeatedly throughout the day, then the task will involve limiting the number of checks to perhaps one time a day. If the behavior is never to allow your son to sleep at a friend's house because you worry about his safety, even though you know and trust the parents of your child's friend, then the practice would be to allow your son to sleep at his friend's house. If one of your anxious behaviors is to never leave the house before everything is clean

Anxious Behaviors Example

Anxious Behavior	Nonanxious Behavior	Anxiety 0–100
Call my spouse several times a day	Call spouse only once a day	50
Arrive at work before anybody else	Arrive at the same time as others	75
Leave work after everybody else	Leave work before others	85
Don't allow my teenage child to sleep over at a friend's	Arrange a sleepover for my child	60
Clean the house every morning in case unexpected guests arrive	Leave the house without cleaning	40
Never delegate projects at work	Delegate a work project	80
Ask for advice from friends and family when making a decision	Make a decision without getting everyone's advice	90
Obtain as much information as I can before making a decision	Make a decision based on less information	85

Anxious Behaviors

Anxious Behavior	Nonanxious Behavior	Anxiety 0–100

and in place, then the practice will be to leave the house with at least one thing left undone. If the behavior is to call a radio station about road accidents to check that your husband is safe and has not been involved in an accident, then the practice will be to prevent yourself from calling the radio station. If the behavior is to stay at work late every night so that your desk is clean and all of the day's tasks are completed, then your practice will be to leave work without cleaning off your desk or completing every task. If your behavior is to avoid inviting friends to your house because you imagine that they will not have a good time, then the task will be to arrange a get-together at your house. If your behavior has been to avoid buying a new car, even though your current car is in terrible condition and you can afford a new car, then the behavioral task will involve taking steps toward purchasing a car and managing the anxiety that will result from decision-making regarding which car to buy. If your anxious behavior involves obtaining excessive amounts of information or opinions from various people about a purchase for fear of making the wrong choice, then the task will involve making the purchase based on fewer opinions and less information. Next to each anxious behavior that you have identified, list the appropriate nonanxious behaviors. Finally, rate each nonanxious behavior on a 0- to 100-point scale on how much anxiety you anticipate you will experience as you practice these nonanxious behaviors. As always, 0 means no anxiety, 50 means a moderate amount of anxiety, and 100 means extreme anxiety.

Of course, your first reaction to these suggestions might be, "I couldn't do that. What if something terrible happens?" Feeling hesitant about these behavioral changes is exactly why it is important to implement them, because the hesitation means that you are continuing to overestimate the likelihood of negative events or continuing to view negative events as unmanageable. Evaluate the likelihood of whatever it is that you are concerned about happening, as well as your ability to deal with the negative event, if it were to happen before you implement the behavioral change. Once you have practiced the behavioral change a number of times, you will learn that whatever it was that you were concerned about either is unlikely or is manageable. The goals are to tolerate imperfection, to let go of attempts to control everything, to let go of the sense of responsibility for unlikely events, and to realize that making mistakes is part of being human. These practices will lead you on a sure path to achieving these goals.

Begin with the least anxiety-provoking behavioral change. Practice this behavioral change as many times as necessary for your anxiety level to decrease to least 25 on the 0- to 100-point scale, in the same way that you did as you faced your most catastrophic images. For example, it may take five days in a row for you to practice not calling the radio station to ask about road accidents before your anxiety about not calling decreases to a mild level. Of course, you should realize by now that your anxiety will decrease with repeated practice because you will learn that your concerns are unfounded; you will gather evidence that allows you to reevaluate the odds and decatastrophize your worries. In other words, by not calling the radio station repeatedly, you will learn that nothing has changed in term of real outcomes, based on whether you call the radio station or not.

You can facilitate these tasks by using cue-controlled relaxation strategies and realistic thinking strategies. For example, if you become very anxious knowing that you left work with one incomplete task on your desk, practice cue-controlled relaxation and consider the real odds of your behavior leading to a serious outcome, and if there is any negative outcome (such as your boss asking why the project was not completed), consider ways in which you would manage it.

As with the imagery exposures, keep a record of your progress with each behavioral change on the Behavioral Change form, as shown in the following example. On the form, record the maximum level of anxiety that you felt during each practice. The form has enough spaces for one behavioral change per day for a week, but you may end up making more changes than one per day; the more, the better. Of course, depending on the task, you may have to wait until the end of the day to make your ratings; that would

Behavioral Change Example

Date	Behavioral Change	Maximum Anxiety (0–100)
Monday 11th	Call husband once only	70
Tuesday 12th	"	60
Wednesday 13th	"	30
Thursday 14th	Not the last to leave office	60
Friday 15th	"	40
Monday 18th	"	25
Tuesday 19th	Arrived at work on time	50

Behavioral Change

Date	Behavioral Change	Maximum Anxiety (0–100)

be the case, for example, if the task were to avoid calling your husband or wife at all when he or she is at work. A summary of the instructions for these behavioral changes is provided.

Instructions for Behavioral Change Exercises

For each behavioral change practice, use the following steps:

1. Consider the practical aspects of the behavioral change: what you must do or not do, and how you will do or not do it. This may entail some planning, such as asking a friend to watch your children, arranging a dinner party, and so on. In addition, inform your family and friends of any changes in behaviors that may affect them. For example, let your husband or wife know if you are not going to make your usual daily calls.

2. Consider the worrisome thoughts that will come to mind as a result of the behavioral change, and think about how you will deal with them. That is, have your realistic thinking strategies prepared to deal with the worry that occurs as you make these behavioral changes.

3. Practice each behavioral change as many times as necessary for your anxiety to decrease to a mild level, about 25 or less on the 0- to 100-point scale. Depending on the task, you may be able to practice it repeatedly very quickly, such as one day after another. For example, limiting yourself to just one phone call to your children or other family members can be practiced every day. On the other hand, some tasks will have to be spread out over longer intervals; for example, arranging for visitors to come to your home or for babysitters to look after your children may be limited to once or twice a week. For this reason, you could tackle several behavioral changes at once, instead of waiting to finish one behavioral change before moving on to the next one. For example, you could leave your desk a mess at the end of the day and ask your supervisor questions that you have been avoiding at the same time. In general, though, it is better to proceed from less anxiety-producing changes to more anxiety-producing changes.

The following difficulties can sometimes occur as you change your behaviors.

1. *Procrastination.* This means putting off the behavioral change with comments such as, "I'll do it next week." Examine the reasons for procrastinating. Maybe you feel that the change is too much work and that it is easier to stay with your old ways. It's true that these behavioral changes require effort and planning, and they will sometimes increase your anxiety. However, the long-term benefit will be worth it. Another reason for procrastination might be that you are afraid to make the behavioral change. In this case, redirect your attention to what you are worried about, how likely that event is, and how you would cope if it were to come true.

2. *Immediate anxiety.* Perhaps you practiced the behavioral change on one occasion and felt so anxious that you decided not to go through with it again. It is possible that you will experience high anxiety the first time you practice some of these behavioral changes because you may feel as if you are setting yourself up for negative outcomes. However, with repeated practice your level of anxiety will decrease. Remember, in the end, it is more effective to take risks than it is to live in a constant state of vigilance and preparation for negative events. Some risk-taking will teach you to be more relaxed and confident in your ability to manage negative events when they do occur.

3. *Being unprepared.* A related difficulty is feeling unprepared to deal with the anxiety that you will experience as a result of the behavioral changes. To be prepared for the anxiety, think of all of the possible worries that could enter your mind as you make these behavioral changes. Then, address each worry by considering the real odds, alternative possibilities, and ways of coping.

4. *Impractical tasks.* Sometimes the behavioral changes are simply too impractical. For example, taking a long trip that you have avoided for years may be very difficult to arrange, in addition to being hard to repeat. It is usually better to work with practical, daily activities, although if the opportunity for a big behavioral change arises, then definitely go for it.

5. *Little or no anxiety.* This may occur because, by the time you reach this point in the program, you already fully understand that you are overestimating the likelihood of negative events or blowing things out of proportion. That is a sign of success. Anxiety also may be minimal if you are "sabotaging" the practice of behavioral change by continuing to engage in subtle safety checks or subtle behavioral avoidances. For example, if the behavioral change is to leave your desk untidy at the end of the day, you may sabotage the goal of learning that a messy desk will not lead to disaster by arriving at work early enough the next day so that you can tidy your desk before anyone else arrives. Watch out for these types of "sabotaging" behaviors.

6. *No decrease in anxiety.* If your anxiety level does not decrease with repeated practice of the behavioral change, it is possible that your thinking is continuing to support the idea of negative outcomes. For example, if visitors did not make negative comments about your home, even though it was not completely in order, you may believe that they simply did not want to tell you how bad it looked, or that they did not notice, but other visitors would have seen the mess, and so on. Of course, these types of interpretations are as negative and unrealistic as the reasons why you have not invited people in the first place. Watch out for these types of misinterpretations.

Homework

✎ Over the next few weeks, tackle the behavioral changes that you have identified.

✎ Record your practices on the Behavioral Change form, and continue to record your daily mood ratings and anxiety episode ratings on the Worry Record.

✎ Continue to apply cue-controlled relaxation and realistic thinking strategies when you notice yourself becoming anxious or tense.

Answer each of the following questions by circling T (true) or F (false). Answers are given in the appendix.

1. If I feel anxious while practicing a behavioral change, it means that I am doing something wrong. T F

2. I should practice each behavioral change the number of times necessary for my anxiety levels to decrease to a mild degree. T F

3. Good behavioral change practice also means good planning. T F

4. It's okay to do more than one behavioral change practice at a time, as long as each one repeated. T F

5. Subtle avoidances and safety checks are okay as long as I perform the basic behavioral change. T F

Chapter 10

Dealing with Real Problems: Time Management, Goal-Setting, and Problem-Solving

Goals

- To review your records from the previous week and add data to your Progress Record

- To learn time management, goal-setting, and problem-solving skills

- To begin to use the Daily Activities form

- To continue record-keeping

- To complete the self-assessment

Review of Your Records

By this point in the program, you should have practiced changing many of your anxious behaviors. If you have not practiced these behavioral changes, we recommend that you spend the time it takes to progress through your list of anxious behaviors before going on.

If you have practiced these behavioral changes, congratulations! Now, ask yourself what you have learned from your behavioral changes. You have probably learned that your initial predictions were incorrect and that your safety-checking or avoidance behaviors were unnecessary. If you still hold on to thoughts, such as, "what if?" or "I was lucky. It could still happen," you will need to further examine the validity of your thoughts. Remember, the purpose of this program is to control excessive worries, not to eliminate appropriate worries about real dangers.

Add your summary data to your Progress Record. Have your ratings declined over time? If so, spend a few minutes thinking about the changes that you've made in the way that you respond to anxiety and worry. Reinforce the benefits of your own hard work by treating yourself to a nice dinner, a movie, or a good book.

Dealing with Problems

As a final step in this training program, we will discuss certain valuable skills that you can use when stressful issues arise. We have found that the most common sources of stress, by far, in our clients, are: (1) feeling overwhelmed by obligations and duties and (2) dealing with crises or problems that arise from time to time in everyone's life. For people who tend to be high-strung or anxious, these stressful situations compound their anxiety. For this reason, we devote this chapter to skills for dealing with these sources of stress. These skills can be divided into time management, goal-setting, and problem-solving through brainstorming.

Time Management

Sometimes people take on too many tasks at one time, often because they feel personally responsible for everything and want everything to be perfect. Of course, having too many tasks creates tension, pressure, and worry about not getting everything done. Ways to deal with this type of stress include: (1) using realistic thinking strategies to address your concerns about what could happen if you did not get everything completed on time and (2) letting go of some of the unnecessary tasks or limiting the number of tasks that you attempt to complete at one time.

To help you determine if you have too many things on your daily schedule right now, make three lists. First, list every activity that you did today, at work and at home. Use the Daily Activities form, as shown in the following example. Be as specific as possible. For example, include all of your routine activities and every task that you spent time on, no matter how big or small. Second, list the activities that you planned to do, but did not do today. Third, list the activities that you wanted to do, but had no time to even consider doing. If the second list is quite long (meaning that you have many things on your schedule that you did not have time to attend to), and if the third list is full of pleasurable activities (meaning that you are someone with too much work and not enough play in your schedule), then you are probably overcommitted. Look at the items on the first list. If some of the items are unnecessary, then it's likely that you are not managing your time very well. Eliminating the unnecessary activities will allow more time for you to complete what you need to do and will also give you some well-deserved time for pleasurable activities.

There are four basic ways to help you manage your time more efficiently.

1. *Delegating responsibility.* It's possible that others in your family or at work could do many of the tasks that you currently perform. For example, instead of making a special trip to the store, you might ask your children or spouse to pick up something from the store on the way home. Similarly, instead of taking primary responsibility for preparing meals, you could ask your children to help. "Fat chance," you may say. A surprisingly large number of our clients don't even bother asking, for fear of conflict and rejection. When they do ask, however, they often get far more help than they anticipated. Remember, if you worry about whether others will do the work as well as you could (which may be one reason why you take on so much work in the first place), you are making predictions that should be subjected to the realistic thinking strategies that we discussed in previous chapters. For example, ask yourself what is the worst that can happen if a letter is not written in exactly the way you would have written it, or if dinner is not cooked as well as you would have cooked it. You can also ask yourself what is the worst that could happen if others find out that you are not taking on all of the responsibilities that you once did.

2. *Saying "no."* It is also possible that you don't complete planned activities because of unexpected demands that you feel obliged to handle.

Daily Activities Example

What I did today Date: Sunday 23rd	What I planned to do, but did not do	What I wanted to do, but did not have time for
Took daughter shopping	Buy new sweater	Take a walk
Cleaned out husband's closet	Clean my desk	Call my sister
Helped daughter with homework	Call my mom	Get manicure
Prepared papers for work tomorrow		Relax
Cooked meals		

Daily Activities Form

What I did today Date: _____	What I planned to do, but did not do	What I wanted to do, but did not have time for

For example, you may have planned to spend several hours working in the garden (an enjoyable and productive activity for you), but your friend called to ask you to baby-sit for her while she goes shopping. Under these circumstances, it is reasonable to say no and not to worry about hurting your friend's feelings. Why? There are two reasons: (1) your friend asked you at the last minute, and (2) it is not a life-or-death situation. Difficulty saying no is often based on worries about being rejected or angering others. Usually, these worries are not based in fact. Saying no and delegating responsibility are very good candidates for the behavioral change exercises that we outlined in the previous chapter. You will most likely find that others will not be hurt if you say no (unless, of course, you say it in a very inappropriate or aggressive manner). Occasionally saying no in an appropriate way can actually contribute to the development of mutual respect between two people.

3. *Sticking to an agenda.* Frequently, we can become overwhelmed by many other tasks that present themselves when we begin one particular assignment. For example, if your task is to organize your files, you might decide to reorganize your entire office. Usually, it is more efficient to stick with the task that you started.

4. *Avoiding perfectionism.* Finally, it is possible that tasks take too long or become overwhelming because of your own perfectionism. In this case, it is important to recognize that raising the bar too high only makes your life more difficult. We often use the 85% rule. If you typically spend 10 hours preparing a document for your office files, this time, spend only 8.5 hours. You must recognize that the document may not be as good as you would have liked, but the importance of the document does not warrant 10 hours of your time. This change requires letting yourself make mistakes and acknowledging imperfection as something that you can tolerate.

Outline for Time Management

1. On the Daily Activities form, write down everything you did during the day in the first column.

2. In the second column, write down every task or activity that you planned to do, but did not do.

3. In the third column, write down every task or activity that you wanted to do, but did not have enough time to do.

4. Look through the entries in the first column, and ask yourself the following questions: Could I have delegated the responsibilities for any of these tasks to my family members, children, or colleagues? Could I have said "no" to doing any of these tasks? Could I have eliminated any of these tasks or activities that were unnecessary by sticking to an agenda? Did I procrastinate, or put off doing any task, by worrying or doing other tasks? Did I spend too much time on any of these tasks because I wanted them to be to perfect?

Goal-Setting

Sometimes, even after using time management skills, we still have too many important things to do, with no chance of completing all of them. At this point, you can just give up and doom yourself to a life of stress and anxiety, or you can set some firm priorities. Setting priorities and realizing that some things just cannot be done is an important skill. Priorities can be set on a daily basis or over the long term. For a given day, make a list of all of the things that you plan to do. Then, decide how important it is to complete each task. To do this, rate each task as A, B, or C. A tasks are top-priority tasks. These are the tasks that absolutely must get done that day. Some days, you may have no A tasks. B tasks are important, but do not absolutely have to get done that day. These are the most common tasks. If they are not completed, they will eventually become A tasks. C tasks need to get done some day, but they aren't really important today.

To organize your day, you can use the following steps. First, record the activities that have to be done at specific times, such as attending meetings, picking up your children, and so on. Then, begin with the A tasks, and schedule them for the times during which you think they can be accomplished. Be somewhat flexible in case you have unexpected interruptions. For example, do not schedule one A task immediately after another A task because you may be interrupted or delayed. You can sacrifice a B or C task so that you can complete an A task, but you cannot sacrifice another A task. Remember to allow much more time to complete the task than you initially predict. Build in time for unexpected events. Next, place the B tasks into some time slots, again giving yourself enough leeway to get them done or partially done. Finally, fill in any remaining time slots with C tasks.

Outline for Goal-Setting

1. For a given day, make a list of all of the things you plan to do.

2. Decide how important it is to complete each activity. Divide the tasks into three categories: A, extremely important, top-priority tasks that must get done today; B, very important tasks that must get done soon, but not necessarily today; and C, important tasks that eventually need to be done, but not very soon.

3. Organize your day by noting all of the activities that must be done at specific times, such as picking up your children from school.

4. Place the A tasks into time slots that allow you enough time and flexibility to get them done.

5. Fill in the other time slots with B tasks, giving yourself enough time and flexibility to get them done.

6. Fill in any remaining time slots with C tasks.

7. If you have an erratic schedule that prevents you from following a daily activity schedule, than make a list of the A, B, and C tasks for the day. Cross each one off after it is done.

Let's take an example from Nancy, one of our clients who had problems with time management, prioritizing tasks, and feeling overwhelmed with real-life problems that occasionally arose. As shown on Nancy's Daily Activities form, which follows, Nancy has a packed day and works long hours as an executive accountant and she also has children. However, some of the activities that she reported on the form were unnecessary. For example, Nancy could have asked her children to clean the cat litter and asked her husband to prepare breakfast (or at least help). That way, she could have done some of the activities in the third column, such as finishing the letter to her sister.

Also, notice how Nancy spent time working on reports and audits as a favor to her co-workers. In the second column, she listed finishing the inventory

Daily Activities Example

What I did today Date: Monday 24th	What I planned to do, but did not do	What I wanted to do, but did not have time for
Cleaned out cat litter	Finish inventory	Aerobics
Cooked breakfast for family	Aerobics	Call friend
Worked on inventory at work	Work on report that is due in 5 days	Finish writing letter to my sister
Did some reports as a favor for a coworker	Speak with supervisor about merit review	Read before bed
Inventory audit		Get my laundry done
Spoke with angry client		Play with kitten
Helped a coworker with an audit		
Dinner interview with a job candidate		
Prepared kids' lunches for next day		
Did husband's laundry		

as something she had wanted to do, but did not do. Clearly, Nancy could have said "no" when asked to do the co-worker's report in order to give herself more time to finish the inventory. Notice that Nancy also spent time on the phone with an angry client. On further questioning, Nancy informed us that this is something that someone else in the office usually handles, but that person was away from his desk. Instead of handling the call herself, Nancy could have not picked up the phone. That would have freed up another hour for her to do other things. Nancy also entertained a job candidate at a restaurant. Once again, Nancy admitted to us that she was asked to do this at the last minute by her supervisor. Normally, Nancy uses this time to go to her aerobics class. Again, Nancy could have delegated the responsibility of the dinner interview to another person. Finally, when Nancy arrived home from work, instead of preparing her kids' lunches for the next day, she could have asked her husband or children to help. We often see this pattern, in which our client takes care of all of the family's needs at the expense of his or her own. This behavior usually stems from wanting things to be perfect and feeling anxious when they are not. Nancy stated to us that her children "are not good at that kind of thing," and said that she has never given them the opportunity to take care of their own lunch preparation. By delegating this job to them, she would not only be giving herself time to relax after work, but also would be teaching her children a valuable skill that they will eventually use. A related issue is Nancy's reluctance to have her husband do his own laundry. She could briefly explain the procedure for washing clothes to him, and then allow him to take care of this task. In this way, she could do her own laundry, read, play with her kitten, and so on—all of the things that she wanted to do, but didn't because she had no time left for herself.

Because her schedule tends to be quite hectic, Nancy decided that the best strategy for reaching her goals would be to make a list of A, B, and C activities for the day. She crossed off each task that she managed to finish that day. Nancy reported that the ABC method of arranging her daily activities helped her to get a sense of what had to get done and what could wait until later. She managed to complete all of her A tasks and also several of her B and C tasks.

Problem-Solving through Brainstorming

Brainstorming is a useful technique for times when real problems or crises arise. Donald Meichenbaum, a Canadian psychologist, has developed a specific set of procedures for helping people solve real problems. Dr. Meichenbaum has found that people tend to have two types of difficulties when problem-solving. First is the tendency to think of the problem in broad, vague, and catastrophic ways. This means becoming overwhelmed and losing sight of the specifics. It is more helpful to think through the specific and objective details of the problem, as opposed to focusing on your thoughts or feelings about the situation. For example, if the problem has to do with your child's rebellious behavior, describing the problem as "Kathy is being very rude" is too vague, while describing the problem as "Kathy doesn't care about my feelings and doesn't appreciate everything that I have done for her over the years" is too emotional. Describing it as "Kathy doesn't do her chores around the house and doesn't tell me what time she will be home" is better, because it is more descriptive and detailed. Part of the skill in problem description is identifying the real problem. For example, if your child is not doing well in school, different solutions would be appropriate, depending on the source of your child's difficulties, such as the teachers, her friends, or her home life.

The second difficulty that many people have when trying to solve problems is feeling that there is no possible solution. This is where brainstorming is used. Brainstorming means letting your mind go and coming up with every possible solution, no matter how unreasonable or silly it may sound. The idea is that, by doing this, you will be more likely to realize that there are potentially good solutions that you had not considered. After you come up with a number of possible solutions, select the solutions that are practical, and then decide which is the best. It is helpful to list the solutions in order of best to worst. Generate several possible solutions so that you have a backup plan if the first one doesn't work. Finally, it's important to decide on a plan of action for carrying out the solution. Following is an outline for brainstorming.

Outline for Brainstorming

When you are faced with a real-life problem or crisis, use the following steps:

1. Write down specifically what the problem is. Avoid being vague, too general, or overly emotional when describing the problem.

2. Let your mind go, and write down every possible solution that comes to you, no matter how foolish, silly, or ridiculous it sounds.

3. Rank these solutions in order, from best to worst, based on how practical and reasonable they are.

4. Decide on a specific plan of action in order to carry out each reasonable solution. Rate the probability of each solution working.

5. Put the plan for the most reasonable solution into action. If it doesn't help to solve the problem, move down your list to the next best solution, and then try again until you can successfully resolve the problem.

While in treatment at our clinic, Michael, one of our clients, complained of having a real-life problem for which he could find no acceptable solution. His problem was car trouble. Michael found himself spending hundreds of dollars on his car's transmission and various engine parts. We suggested that

Brainstorming Example: *Spending Too Much Money on an Old Car*

Possible solutions	Rank order of how practical/ reasonable (1 = best)	Probability of solution working (0%–100%)
Trade it in and buy a new car	3	100
Go to a different mechanic	1	95
Buy a used car	4	70
Sue the car company	6	10
Take out a loan and buy a brand new engine and transmission	5	60
Trade in the car, then borrow my brother's car until I have saved enough money for a new car	2	90
Deliberately burn it or total it, and collect insurance money	7	2

he try brainstorming to find a solution. The results of his brainstorming session are shown in the table. Clearly, the best thing that Michael could do at this point was get a second opinion about his car from a different mechanic. Perhaps all his car needed was better service and maintenance. "Going to a different mechanic" would be the best solution to try first.

Michael listed his second best solution as borrowing his brother's car after trading in his own car and saving up for a new car. Michael planned to use this solution if another mechanic also said that his car needed serious work. Using what is called a cost-benefit analysis, or a closer look at the expenses associated with both short-term and long-term solutions, Michael realized that the money he was spending on repairs totaled more than the cost of buying a new, reliable car, with few maintenance problems. It would be practical to trade in or sell his current car and borrow his brother's extra car while Michael saved for a new one. As we see from Michael's ratings, he used this cost-benefit analysis to judge how reasonable and practical each solution would be. The seventh best solution in which he would deliberately burn or total the car and collect the insurance money, is, for obvious reasons, the least desirable possibility and a rather extreme and criminal way to solve this problem! Brainstorming, then, can help you gain a sense of perspective on your real-life problems and pave the way for solving them.

Now, let's examine Michael's probability rating. Although he rated "trade it in and buy a new car" as having 100% probability of working, his first choice, "go to a different mechanic," was the least expensive and most beneficial strategy to try at this point, even though it may not be as effective as buying a new car. Since Michael, like most people, must live on a budget, he used the cost-benefit analysis to find the best solution with a high probability of working.

Homework

✎ Choose some problems that have been bothering you lately, and try the brainstorming technique described in this chapter.

✎ Use the time management strategies every day for the next week.

✎ Continue monitoring your anxiety using the Daily Mood Record and the Worry Record.

Self-Assessment

Answer each of the following questions by circling T (true) or F (false). Answers are given in the appendix.

1. Brainstorming means to generate all of the solutions that come to mind, regardless of how ridiculous they seem. T F

2. Setting goals involves placing tasks in the categories of extremely important, very important, and important. T F

3. Dealing with real problems is best done by questioning the real odds and decatastrophizing. T F

4. Time pressure can stem from an unrealistic sense of responsibility and from being overcommitted to too many tasks. T F

Chapter 11

Drugs for Anxiety and Their Relation to This Program

Goals

◾ To learn about the different medications that can be used to help treat anxiety

◾ To talk to your physician about stopping your medication, if you are currently taking any

Reasons for Taking Drugs for Anxiety

If you're like many people with anxiety, you have probably already been to see your family doctor, who has prescribed a mild tranquilizer for your anxiety. You may be taking this medication regularly, or perhaps only occasionally, when you feel particularly nervous or anxious. Many people go through this program without ever taking medication; others would just as soon not take the medication, but are doing so on the advice of their physician. However, there are a number of people who take medication for their anxiety, for a variety of reasons. For some, the anxiety is so overwhelmingly severe that they feel that they cannot take even one more day of being anxious, and they want relief as soon as possible. Even the drug that takes the longest time to start to be effective would take only three weeks. Some of the shorter-acting drugs can be effective within a day or two. These drugs are likely to have some beneficial effect in a shorter period than this program, unless you are able to set aside time to work through the chapters fairly quickly. Others may not feel that they have the time to devote to this program right now, and believe that medication is the next best option. Still others may believe strongly that medication is the most appropriate treatment for their anxiety.

In any case, almost 60% of the people who come to one of our clinics for treatment are taking some kind of medication for their anxiety. Naturally, all of the people coming to our clinics who are taking medication are still suffering from anxiety, or they wouldn't bother to come. For others, their family physician has given them a prescription to get through the next couple of weeks, but has also told them to come to our clinics as soon as possible.

As we mentioned in the introduction, it is not at all necessary that you stop taking your medication before starting the program. However, approximately half of the people completing this program stop taking drugs on their own (usually with the help of their physician) by the time they finish this program, and most others stop sometime during the first year after they finish the program. Below, we describe methods for using this program to help you stop taking drugs, if you want to.

At this point, the evidence seems quite clear that several types of drugs, if prescribed at the appropriate dosage, may be effective for at least short-term relief of anxiety for some people. Many of these drugs, however, are not effective in the long term unless you continue to take them indefinitely. Even then, they may lose some of their effectiveness, unless you learn some new, more adaptive methods of coping with your anxiety while you are taking the drug.

There are also some individuals who begin drug therapy and stop several months later, without any need to go through a program such as this. Whether the particular stress that they were under has resolved itself, whether there were some neurobiological changes in their "emotional sensitivity," or whether they developed a different attitude toward their anxiety, that was the only treatment that they needed. For all of these reasons, it seems useful to review briefly the types of medications prescribed for anxiety, as well as the best times to use them, based on current knowledge.

Anti-Anxiety Drugs

Benzodiazepines, or high-potency benzodiazepines, better known as minor tranquilizers, are commonly prescribed for anxiety. The types and brand names of minor tranquilizers are far too numerous to mention here, but four of the most common are diazepam (Valium), alprazolam (Xanax), lorazepam (Ativan), and clonazepam (Klonopin). There is another type of anti-anxiety drug that is not a benzodiazepine. This drug is called buspirone (BuSpar). The U.S. Food and Drug Administration (FDA) has approved all of these drugs, except klonopin, for the treatment of GAD.

Typically, these drugs are prescribed for short-term relief of anxiety. Evidence indicates that these drugs can be effective in relieving anxiety for a short period, although there is little or no evidence that they work over a long period. One of the reasons for this is that after several weeks, a tolerance to some of these drugs begins to develop. That is, you would require a higher dosage of the drug to obtain the same anxiety-reducing effect. Also, unless you work carefully with your doctor, there is a danger that you could become psychologically and physically dependent on benzodiazepines. If dependence does develop, it can be very hard to stop taking the drug because you will experience some withdrawal effects. In other words, you will very quickly feel the symptoms of anxiety that the drug relieved, but many of these symptoms could be due to the effects of withdrawing from the drug. Finally, many people relapse when they stop taking benzodiazepines. For all of these reasons, you should work very closely with your doctor as you cut back on using the drug.

BuSpar does not seem to have many of the problems with dependence and withdrawal found with the benzodiazepines, but it is the impression of many physicians that its anxiety-reducing effects are not as strong, either. Since very few research studies have been done, we can't say for sure what the effects are. In any case, many doctors recommend anti-anxiety drugs only for short-term relief during a particularly anxious period. The purpose of the drugs would be to help you get through a difficult situation. After the situation is resolved, you would stop taking the drug so that you would not become dependent on it.

Antidepressant Drugs with Anxiety-Reducing Properties

There is wide agreement that antidepressant drugs that have anxiety-reducing properties are the first choice in drug treatment for GAD. The most popular of these drugs are the selective serotonin reuptake inhibitors (SSRIs), as well as the serotonin-norepinephrine reuptake inhibitors (SNRIs). Most of these drugs seem approximately equal in effectiveness for GAD, particularly when combined with the type of program presented in this book. The major difficulty with these drugs is that they can take three weeks or more to be effective, and you may experience some relatively minor side effects during that three-week period, which, to some people, seem very similar to anxiety. A more important and widespread side effect of these drugs is sexual dysfunction. Nevertheless, all things considered, these drugs are the best choice at this time for GAD. Drugs of this type that have been approved by the FDA for the treatment of GAD include paroxetine (Paxil), venlafaxine (Effexor), and escitalopram (Lexapro). Both Paxil and Effexor come in extended-release tablets, which means that you can take fewer pills per day. Recommended starting dosages of each of these drugs, as well as the dosage range (which means the amount of drug that you would want to be taking to get the full therapeutic effects), are listed in table 11.1. If you are taking one of these drugs, but not within the recommended dosage range, you may want to check with your doctor to find out why. He or she may have a good reason, but sometimes doctors are reluctant to prescribe a higher dosage of a drug, even though all of the research shows that you really don't get the benefit from the drug outside of the therapeutic dosage range. Some other antidepressant drugs with anxiety-reducing properties that probably have similar effects, but have not been approved by the FDA for the treat-

Table 11.1. Drug Treatments for Generalized Anxiety Disorder[a]

Medication	Brand name	Initial dose (mg/day)	Dose range (mg/day)
FDA–approved drugs for GAD			
Paroxetine (SSRI)	Paxil	10	10–50
Escitalopram (SSRI)	Lexapro	10	10–20
Venlafaxine XR (SNRI)	Effexor	37.5	73–300
Alprazolam (benzodiazepine)	Xanax	1	2–10
Lorazepam (benzodiazepine)	Ativan	0.75	3–10
Diazepam (benzodiazepine)	Valium	4	4–40
Buspirone (azapirone)	BuSpar	15	15–60
Not approved by FDA at this time for GAD			
Fluoxetine (SSRI)	Prozac	5–10	10–80
Sertraline (SSRI)	Zoloft	25	25–200
Citalopram (SSRI)	Celexa	10	20–60
Fluvoxamine (SSRI)	Luvox	25	25–300
Clomipramine (TCA)	Anafranil	25	25–250
Imipramine (TCA)	Tofranil	75	50–200
Clonazepam (benzodiazepine)	Klonopin	0.25	1–5

[a]Modified from Goodman (2004).

Abbreviations: FDA, U.S. Food and Drug Administration; GAO, generalized anxiety disorder; SNRI, serotonin-norepinephrine reuptake inhibitor; SSRI, selective serotonin reuptake inhibitor; TCA, tricyclic antidepressant.

ment of GAD, mostly because the companies making them have not yet submitted these drugs for approval, are also listed in table 11.1. The drugs that you have most likely heard of include fluoxetine (Prozac), sertraline (Zoloft), citalopram (Celexa), and fluvoxamine (Luvox). Once again, these drugs are probably just about as effective as the drugs approved by the FDA, but some individuals tolerate one of these drugs better than another, and sometimes your doctor will need to try several different drugs to find out which one is best for you.

Sometimes, an older class of antidepressant medications, tricyclic antidepressants, is prescribed for anxiety, including drugs such as imipramine (Tofranil) and clomipramine (Anafranil). The effectiveness of these drugs is approximately equal to that of the SSRI or SNRI drugs mentioned earlier, but they seem to have more side effects for some people, and the side effects strongly resemble anxiety. Although the side effects stop after two to three weeks, many people have trouble getting through that period. It is much easier to stop taking these drugs than it is to stop taking the benzodiazepines. Nevertheless, relapse rates approach 50% in the six months after discontinuation of the drug.

Beta-Blockers

Many people take beta-blockers in order to reduce their blood pressure or regulate their heart rate. These drugs act on a specific receptor, the beta-receptor, which is involved in physiological arousal. Therefore, if one needs to avoid physiological arousal for medical reasons, beta-blockers are often prescribed. Again, there are a large number of beta-blockers available, but the most popular is propranolol (Inderal). One would think that any medication that reduces arousal, which is so much a part of anxiety, would have some beneficial effect. Nevertheless, there is very little, if any, evidence that Inderal is useful in any way for anxiety, although occasionally, someone might feel a little better. For that reason, psychiatrists who are knowledgeable about the drug treatment of anxiety almost never prescribe this drug to treat anxiety.

Stopping Your Drug Use

Now that you have completed this program, you should be ready to stop your medication if you want to. Chances are you already have done so. If not, be very sure that you stop taking your medication under the supervision of your physician; only he or she can decide how soon it will be safe for you to taper your medication to the point where you eliminate it altogether. This will be particularly true for drugs (such as Xanax) that are very hard to stop taking. Nevertheless, with what you have learned from this program, you should have little trouble stopping your medication if you follow these guidelines.

1. Withdraw from your medication relatively slowly. Don't try to do it all at once. Once again, your doctor will be able to give you the best advice on what rate (schedule) of withdrawal is appropriate for you.

2. Set a target date for stopping your medication altogether. Once again, this will have to be planned with your physician, so make it a reasonable date, in view of your own withdrawal (tapering) schedule. On the other hand, the date should not be too far away. Generally, the quicker, the better, as long as it is within a schedule that is reasonable for you, as determined by your physician.

3. Use the principles and coping skills that you have learned in this program as you withdraw from the medication.

The reason that we have not addressed this topic until now is because it is important for you to learn how to master your anxiety and worry before successfully stopping your medication. One of the major reasons for this is that you may begin to experience anxiety at somewhat more intense levels as you withdraw from medication, particularly if you were taking minor tranquilizers. If you were never taking medication, then you have mastered your anxiety by now. If you are taking medication, the principles you have learned may need to be applied again as you experience some anxiety when you stop your medication. Once again, most people do not find this a problem, and generally reduce their medication use as they become more comfortable in dealing with their anxiety using this program. These people never experience a series of new outbreaks of anxiety as they withdraw from their medication. However, if, for some reason, your anxiety seems to be increasing, particularly if you are withdrawing from one of the benzodiazepines, you should be reassured by the fact that this will only last a week or two, at most, until the drug clears from your system. In addition, you now have the skills to handle this anxiety, and perhaps eliminate it entirely.

If withdrawal from benzodiazepines or other medications is posing a particular problem in your life, and is something you have tried before, unsuccessfully, while working with your physician, then the book *Stopping Anxiety Medication* may be useful for you. That particular program is designed specifically for panic attacks, as well as symptoms of very severe anxiety and panic that one feels when attempting to withdraw from benzodiazepines or other drugs.

Homework

✎ If you are currently taking medication and wish to stop taking it, then your assignment for this week is to speak with your doctor about the best way to do it.

✎ Plan how you will deal with any of the anxiety-inducing effects or drug withdrawal by using the various strategies and principles described in the previous chapters. Draw up a specific step-by-step plan for yourself.

Chapter 12   *Your Accomplishments and Your Future*

Goals

▨ To evaluate your progress by using the Self-Evaluation form

▨ To determine the next step

▨ To consider methods of maintaining your progress

▨ To consider potential high-risk situations for the future

Self-Evaluation

It's time to consider the kinds of changes that you have made since you first began this program, using the Self-Evaluation form. Change is most accurately assessed by using actual ratings and recordings, as summarized in your Progress Report. Compare the frequency of anxiety episodes per week, from the first week of monitoring until the last week of monitoring (that is, now). There may be ups and downs, which is very typical. However, if you have experienced what you consider to be a significant reduction in the number of anxiety episodes, check the "Yes" box next to the item labeled "Number of anxiety episodes" on your Self-Evaluation form. If the number of episodes has not reduced or has increased, check the "No" box. Similarly, examine the maximum anxiety ratings for each week, from the beginning of monitoring to the end of monitoring. If you have experienced what you consider to be a significant reduction in how anxious you are during the day, check the "Yes" box next to the item labeled "Maximum daily anxiety." If your average maximum anxiety ratings have not changed, or have increased, check the "No" box.

Next, think about the catastrophic images that you repeatedly faced in chapter 8. Compare your initial anxiety ratings with the level of anxiety that you now experience when imagining these scenes. If your anxiety level

Self-Evaluation

	Yes	No
Number of anxiety episodes	_____	_____
Maximum daily anxiety	_____	_____
Catastrophic images	_____	_____
Anxious behaviors	_____	_____

has reduced, check the "Yes" box next to the item labeled "Catastrophic images." Check "No" if your anxiety in relation to these images has not decreased.

Finally, consider the list of behavioral changes that you identified as ways of replacing anxious behaviors. Rate your level of anxiety now for each behavioral change. If your level of anxiety is significantly less than when you first rated those behavioral changes (chapter 9), check the "Yes" box next to the item labeled "Anxious behaviors"; if not, check "No."

If you have checked the "Yes" box for at least two of the four items, then you have progressed very well with this program. If, on the other hand, you have checked "No" to three or more of the items, then there is still room for gains to be made.

What to Do Next

On the basis of your Self-Evaluation, decide whether you have responded well to the program or whether you have room to make more improvements. If you feel good about your level of progress, then your strategy should be to identify any remaining areas of concern and to continue with the same principles and strategies that you have been taught up until this point. Think of any remaining difficulties with the way you react to events (any tendencies to overestimate the risk or to catastrophize), repetitive worries that you find bothersome and difficult to get rid of, or excessive caution in your behavior. Review the appropriate chapters to help you with these remaining areas.

If, on the other hand, you decide that you still have a long way to go, evaluate the following possible reasons why you may not have done as well with the program as you would have liked:

The initial decision that this program was appropriate for you may not have been accurate. This is likely the case if you found that much of the material in the program did not seem relevant to the kinds of problems that you are encountering. In this case, you should discuss with your doctor or mental health professional the need for further assessment to identify a more appropriate program.

Some people simply need a longer time to complete the program, depending on various factors. Requiring a longer time is not an indication of lack of success with the program, but simply an indication of the need for continued application of the strategies, as described. This possibility would be most likely if you have experienced some improvement, although not as much as you would like. If so, continue applying the strategies. If absolutely no progress has been made, then the first possibility may be more likely.

The program is appropriate, but the amount of effort you have put in has not been sufficient. This is the most common reason for lack of success. Have you practiced regularly and sufficiently? Perhaps events have occurred that have taken your attention away from the program (such as a family crisis or marital problems). If so, the success of the program simply depends on renewed effort and motivation. If motivation is a more general issue (you have not practiced regularly, despite having the time to do so), then it may he better to stop the and return to it when you are feeling more motivated.

The fourth possibility is that you have not fully understood the major principles of this program. In this case, a review of all of the principles, preferably with the help of your doctor or mental health professional, is suggested.

Finally, lack of success may be a function of the way in which you are defining success. Remember, success is change in the right direction, no matter how small. If you are waiting for a time when you feel absolutely no anxiety, worry, or tension, you are most likely using unrealistic standards of success. Change is gradual, and some anxiety is necessary.

If you have done well with this program, or are still in the process of achieving control by continued use of the strategies, one issue to keep in mind is how to maintain, or keep up, the changes that you have made. Sometimes people ask, "Will I always be anxious?" or "Has this program simply taught me how to suppress an underlying anxiety that will always be part of me?" To respond to the first question, it is important to remember that anxiety is a perfectly normal human trait; all of us experience anxiety, and in fact, as we discussed earlier, it would be unadaptive to completely remove anxiety from our lives because it plays such a big role in motivation for performance. Learning to control excessive levels of anxiety is like any other learned behavior; once the way to achieve control is learned, then that behavior becomes more powerful with time. However, there are some situations that may increase the likelihood of experiencing high levels of anxiety in the future (discussed below).

To respond to the second question, it is important to understand that the goal of this program is not to suppress anxiety. Instead, the methods you have been taught are intended to change the way you react so that you no longer experience excessive anxiety. You are learning to reach the core of your anxiety reactions and to change them. Always keep in mind that anxiety is an emotional response that is made up of certain key features and processes, such as physical arousal, patterns of thought, and avoidance behaviors. By changing these components of your anxiety response, your anxiety itself is changed.

Certain key factors will promote the continuation of the accomplishments that you've made during the program. First, whenever you notice yourself worrying about something over and over again, or worrying to the extent that it is difficult to stop, use this as a signal to evaluate your thoughts. Take a step out of the anxiety cycle to examine what you are saying to yourself, how likely it is, and what is the worst that can happen. Remember to become an observer rather than a victim. Second, if you notice physical tension building in your body, such as headaches or backaches, practice the relaxation strategy. Finally, watch out for the subtle behaviors that are based on worrisome thoughts, such as watching for news stories about car accidents, and so on. In summary, act on your signals of anxiety, worry, and tension, rather than letting them take over your whole being. It is helpful, and generally a good idea, to review the material in the various chapters on occasion.

Also, don't view an episode of high anxiety as evidence or loss of all of the gains that you've made. That's the time when you must become an objective observer, outside of the bowl of gelatin, examining the reasons why you became so anxious, so that the appropriate strategies for anxiety management can be applied.

High-Risk Times

From our work, we have found that the likelihood of experiencing high levels of anxiety again increases at times when you experience a lot of stress. This might include positive stress (such as a job promotion or having a new baby) or negative stress (such as losing someone close to you). High levels of stress might lead you to feel more physical tension, since you are likely to be more physically aroused. Along with the physical tension, you might experience an increase in your worry. The key is to remember the strategies for dealing with the worry and tension.

References

American Psychiatric Association. (1994). *Diagnostic and Statistical Manual of Mental Disorders,* 4th ed. Washington, DC: Author.

Barlow, D. H. (2002). *Anxiety and its disorders: The nature and treatment of anxiety and panic.* New York: Guilford Press.

Butler, G., & Mathews, A. (1983). Cognitive process in anxiety. *Advances in Behavior Research and Therapy, 5,* 51–62.

Goodman, W. K. (2004). Selecting pharmacotherapy for generalized anxiety disorder. *Journal of Clinical Psychiatry, 65,* 8–13.

Otto, M. W., Pollack, M. H., & Barlow, D. H. (1995). *Stopping anxiety medication: Panic control therapy for benzodiazepine discontinuation.* New York: Oxford University Press.

Van Meter, S.A., & Doraiswamy, P.M. (2001). Anxiety disorders. In P. E. Rakel & E.T. Bope (Eds.), *Conn's Current Therapy* (pp. 1137–1142). Philadelphia: W.B. Saunders Company.

About the Authors

Michelle G. Craske received her Ph.D. from the University of British Columbia in 1985, and has published over 160 articles and chapters in the area of anxiety disorders. She has written books on the topics of the etiology and treatment of anxiety disorders, gender differences in anxiety, and translation from the basic science of fear learning to the clinical application of understanding and treating phobias, in addition to several self-help books. In addition, she has been the recipient of continuous National Institute of Mental Health funding since 1991 for research projects pertaining to risk factors for anxiety disorders and depression among children and adolescents, the cognitive and physiological aspects of anxiety and panic attacks, and the development and dissemination of treatments for anxiety and related disorders. She is Associate Editor of the *Journal of Abnormal Psychology and Behaviour Research and Therapy,* and is a Scientific Board Member for the Anxiety Disorders Association of America. She was a member of the *DSM-IV* Anxiety Disorders Work Group Subcommittee for revision of the diagnostic criteria for panic disorder and specific phobia. Dr. Craske has given invited keynote addresses at many international conferences and frequently is invited to present training workshops on the most recent advances in cognitive-behavioral treatment of anxiety disorders. She is currently a Professor in the Department of Psychology and Department of Psychiatry and Biobehavioral Sciences, University of California, Los Angeles (UCLA), and Director of the UCLA Anxiety Disorders Behavioral Research Program.

David H. Barlow received his Ph.D. from the University of Vermont in 1969 and has published over 500 articles and chapters, including nearly 50 books and clinical workbooks, mostly in the area of emotional disorders and clinical research methods. The book and workbooks have been translated into more than 20 languages, including Arabic, Mandarin, and Russian.

He was formerly Professor of Psychiatry at the University of Mississippi Medical Center and Professor of Psychiatry and Psychology at Brown University, and he founded clinical psychology internships in both settings. He was also Distinguished Professor in the Department of Psychology at the University at Albany, State University of New York. Currently, he is Professor of Psychology, Research Professor of Psychiatry, and Director of the Center for Anxiety and Related Disorders at Boston University.

Dr. Barlow is the recipient of the 2000 American Psychological Association (APA) Distinguished Scientific Award for the Applications of Psychology. He is also the recipient of the First Annual Science Dissemination Award from the Society for a Science of Clinical Psychology of the APA and recipient of the 2000 Distinguished Scientific Contribution Award from the Society of Clinical Psychology of the APA. He also received an award in appreciation for outstanding achievements from the General Hospital of the Chinese People's Liberation Army, Beijing, China, with an appointment as Honorary Visiting Professor of Clinical Psychology. During the 1997–1998 academic year, he was Fritz Redlich Fellow at the Center for Advanced Study in Behavioral Sciences, in Palo Alto, California.

Other awards include Career Contribution Awards from the Massachusetts, California, and Connecticut Psychological Associations; the 2004 C. Charles Burlingame Award from the Institute of Living in Hartford, Connecticut; the First Graduate Alumni Scholar Award from the Graduate College, the University of Vermont; the Masters and Johnson Award, from the Society for Sex Therapy and Research; G. Stanley Hall Lectureship, APA; a certificate of appreciation for contributions to women in clinical psychology from Section IV of Division 12 of the APA, the Clinical Psychology of Women; and a MERIT award from the National Institute of Mental Health for long-term contributions to the clinical research effort. He is Past-President of the Society of Clinical Psychology of the APA and the Association for the Advancement of Behavior Therapy; Past-Editor of the journals *Behavior Therapy, Journal of Applied Behavior Analysis,* and *Clinical Psychology: Science and Practice;* and currently Editor-in-Chief of the "Treatments that Work™" series for Oxford University Press.

He was Chair of the APA Task Force of Psychological Intervention Guidelines, a member of the *DSM-IV* Task Force of the American Psychiatric Association, and a Co-Chair of the Work Group for revising the anxiety disorder categories. He is also a Diplomate in Clinical Psychology of the American Board of Professional Psychology, and maintains a private practice.

Appendix   *Answers to Self-Assessment Quizzes*

Chapter 2

1. T   3. T
2. F

Chapter 3

1. T   4. F
2. T   5. T
3. F

Chapter 4

1. F   4. F
2. T   5. F
3. T   6. T

Chapter 5

1. T   4. T
2. F   5. F
3. T

Chapter 6

1. T   4. F
2. T   5. T
3. F

Chapter 7

1. F   4. F
2. T   5. T
3. T

Chapter 8

1. F   4. F
2. F   5. F
3. T

Chapter 9

1. F
2. T
3. T
4. T
5. F

Chapter 10

1. T
2. T
3. F
4. T